John T. Teat

The Farmer's Garden, and Its Management

John T. Teat

The Farmer's Garden, and Its Management

ISBN/EAN: 9783337083342

Printed in Europe, USA, Canada, Australia, Japan

Cover: Foto ©Lupo / pixelio.de

More available books at **www.hansebooks.com**

...The...

Farmer's Garden,

AND ITS MANAGEMENT.

A Practical Guide to Successful Gardening,

WITH

Notes On Injurious Insects,

THE LAWN

And the Culture of Flowers,

...BY...
JNO. T. TEAT.
1896-8.

COPYRIGHTED, 1898,
BY
JNO. T. TEAT,
CARDINGTON, OHIO.

Author's Preface.

In writing this treatise, it has been the author's earnest endeavor to treat the subject chosen in a plain, practical and concise manner, easily understood by all.

While aware of the fact that there are many excellent works on the "garden and its management," a great many of them do not meet the requirements of the beginner, they being written in too professional a manner, not easily understood by those who are young in this pleasant and profitable employment—gardening.

The author believes this work will be found complete in its way, simple in construction, plain and practical, and trusts it will be of assistance to you in supplying your requirements; and, too, we hope you will find some interest in its pages whether you are an amateur or a professional. Such has been our earnest endeavor, and we trust it will be recognized as a trustworthy guide.

After a careful study of its pages, even the most inexperienced should be able to care for the Kitchen Garden, be it an acre, or more, or less. And as a beautiful, well-kept lawn, with its beds of flowers, adds much to the attractiveness of rural as well as city homes, we have added notes on the preparation of the one and the culture of the other, so that you may not only be supplied with an abundance of the finest vegetables and fruits, but also enjoy the delights of home life through its surrounding attractions.

The notes given on the care of the lawn and the culture of flowers are fully as trustworthy as those given on the care of the Garden, and if followed, success will be reasonably assured.

And now, kind reader, we commend it to your care, hoping you will make an aquaintance agreeable to all. So, wishing you great success in your labors, we beg to remain your faithful and humble servant,

JOHN T. TEAT.

CARDINGTON, O., Jan. 3, '96.

"Gardening is an occupation for which no man is too high nor too low."

The Farmer's Garden

And Its Management.

INTRODUCTORY.

THE GARDEN is generally regarded as one of the most insignificant parts of the farm—frequently more of a nuisance than anything else—only to be tolerated to satisfy the whims of the "wimen folks," while if cared for as it should be we would find it to be one of the most profitable plots of ground on the farm. So firmly grounded is this nuisance idea in the masculine mind that no effort is made to cultivate a really good one, and thereby ascertain the real value of a generous supply of crisp and delicious vegetables on the table throughout the year. Do not be content with raising the common varieties only, but have a place for everything and everything in its place.

This not being the case, we may be pardoned for scolding a little and for taking the part of the too often sadly neglected farmer's garden, when it should be a tempting feature of every home. There is no country in the world capable of producing a greater or better supply of table "sass" than is ours. Every family in the land should be constantly supplied with the best vegetables and fruits, which is of great advantage to health, and reduces the grocer's, butcher's and doctor's bills. In writing this treatise we shall endeavor to give a few practical points to aid you in making a start.

The limited number of vegetable and fruit gardens worthy of the name found in connection with rural homes is really astonishing when it is remembered that the farmer has facilities for gardening, if properly used, to distance all competition, and thereby not only improve the health of his own family but also add many a dollar to his income. He has his choice of soil as well as fertilizers and ample horse power to aid him in tilling the soil; and yet, of all gardens, the farmer's garden is too often the most sadly neglected and valueless.

Quite true, farm life is very busy at the season of the year when the garden calls for attention, and this is perhaps the reason for the neglect shown in the farmer's garden. The family of the town can find a supply on the market but this is quite often of inferior quality; but the farmer's family often has to go without even these, when the very best of everything could be had in abundance throughout the year by a little effort being put forth on the part of the farmer. All quick-maturing crops require much richer soil than those that require a longer season in which to reach maturity. Late peas, like marrowfats, etc., will yield a good crop on moderately rich soil, without manure, while the early varieties that mature in May require an abundance of plant food easily available early in the season. The same is true of most all, if not all, crops; the shorter the time in which they mature the better chance they must have.

In all crops that require to be thinned, every day's neglect after the plants are large enough to thin reduces the crop. This work should be done promptly as soon as you can get hold of them with thumb and finger. The same is true of all delicate crops that require hand-weeding as they should be cleaned out as soon as the row can be seen. A delay of a few days or even hours will double the work and the loss of a week's time may ruin the crop; then, too, a wet spell may give the weeds such a start that it will be impossible to save the crop.

The time to destroy weeds is before they come up, while the mere stirring of the soil as soon as dry enough after a rain destroys most of the weeds that have started, besides giving your crop a start over the few weeds that may be left. Make it a rule that no weed, no, not even the finest specimen, shall go to seed on your garden, or better still, on your farm. The average garden ripens enough noxious seeds every season to supply the entire community. Judgment must be used in covering seeds of various kinds, and the amount of soil and compacting must be regulated according to the season.

Seeds sown early require light covering and little or no pressing of the soil, while midsummer planting requires more soil over them, which should be packed firmly about them.

All crops which come up small and require hand-weeding should be sown in straight and very narrow drills. If a crooked furrow is made it will require very much more hand-weeding to keep them clean, compared to what there is when a straight drill one inch wide receives the seed.

Where land is to grow a second crop, as in the case of early peas, beans, spinach, potatoes, etc., everything should be on hand to do the work at once and take advantage of suitable weather that may come. All work must be done promptly and at just the right time or the labor will be greatly increased.

In nearly all cases the hoe and the rake can be used to advantage before the seeds come up, and right over the row, too, if carefully used. The weeds will thus be kept in check and the moisture retained for the future use of the crop.

I rather like the idea of keeping the ground covered with vegetation throughout the season, as there will be more encouragement to keep it clean and in the very best condition, and looking its very prettiest. Whenever possible sow a crop of rye for plowing under in the spring, if the plowing is not done in the fall. Or sow it anyway.

The Location.

The kitchen garden should be located as near the house as possible and should not be located on another road half a mile from the house, thereby compelling the "gude" wife to travel all over a quarter-section every time she wishes a few vegetables for dinner or supper. But when located near the house it should be enclosed by a poultry tight fence, or I am afraid someone will say something not suited for publication; for "biddy" seems to know just where the hills are that contain the choicest varieties. In choosing a location I would prefer a plot in the shape of a parallelogram; that is, about twice as long as wide, provided the land that can be appropriated admits of this shape.

This plot should contain about an acre, more or less, to suit your own individual requirements; but an acre will give sufficient space for everything from radishes, onions, lettuce, etc., to potatoes, corn and small fruits. On the outside next the boundaries a border of about ten feet wide should be left for the growing of the smaller vegetables; on the sunny side, those that mature early in the season and on the northernly side those varieties that require shade.

Before going farther, I will say that the garden should be as nearly level as possible, or if sloping, not so much so as to be in danger of being washed by heavy rains. If sloping, it should be toward the south or east, and should be so situated as to have a good surface drainage, for without this, or under-draining, it is almost impossible to raise early or fine vegetables at a profit.

These are to be considered the most essential points in selecting a plot for a garden. Of course, a rich soil is to be desired, but if that is deficient the gardener can, by the use of manure, remedy a deficiency of this kind in a few seasons, while he cannot make a favorable location for early vegetables on a north slope if he should endeavor to do so for a lifetime. If it were possible, I would have no fence around the garden, as it is usually more of a nuisance than anything else, being overgrown with weeds, and a waste of ground where it is not a necessity. But if a fence is necessary, have a good one so as to keep out poultry as well as stock.

The gardener has no use for a scratching hen, cats, dogs, etc., in his beds of plants, for these are his most aggravating enemies. A scratching hen seems to know just where the choicest seeds are planted, while cats and dogs like to roll in a bed of plants.

In plowing the ground in early spring I would not plow more than is needed for the first planting, and the remainder when the soil has become more dry and friable, as it will not then become packed by the heavy spring rains which are sure to come about this time of the year. For the first planting the ground should be plowed and the seeds sown as soon as the ground can be prepared; the hardier varieties such as peas, radishes, onions and lettuce, will even stand a slight frost, and while adapting their growth to the weather will be ready to smile a welcome on the first warm spring days.

Sometimes we cannot wait for the soil to be in the very best condition, as in a drought, when we wish to plant a second crop. In this case it must be brought into as fine a condition as possible, by rolling and harrowing. The former is often neglected in the average garden.

The small fruits should all be on one side of the garden where they will not interfere with the working of the rest of the garden in spring or fall. In planting, the width of the cultivator and swingle-tree must be taken into consideration.

If the soil has been heavily manured, the rows may be planted as closely as will admit of cultivation and allow a good supply of sun and air to reach the roots, excepting melons, cucumbers, squashes, etc., which should have ample room to make a spread and sun themselves.

Bush beans, dwarf peas, etc., can be sown as closely as two feet, while corn, pole beans and other tall-growing crops should be at least three feet apart each way, while small-growing crops such as onions, lettuce, radishes, spinach, etc., can be sown as closely as one foot apart, not only to admit of working but to allow sun and air to reach the roots.

The Soil of the Garden.

Soil on which some cultivated crop has been grown is preferable to sod for starting a garden, as it is more easily brought into a fine condition in early spring. Another fault is that grass is also one of the hardest weeds to destroy among small crops such as onions and radishes. Sod is also often infested with grubs, which prey upon young tomato, cabbage and vine plants. Whether new land, or in the old garden, it is best to put all coarse manure on in the fall and plow it under as soon as the ground can be cleared.

The land should be plowed in the fall and left as plowed. A plow with a straight mould board should be used for fall plowing, as it leaves the moulds more on edge and therefore more to the action of the frost, which will be of great benefit to heavy soils that are late in drying out in the spring, which is of great advantage, as every kind of products can be gotten in when the proper season arrives, while it also adds much to the appearance of the garden. A few days too late may mean failure. The gases arising from the decaying of the manure also tends to lighten the soil instead of being wasted in the air, as when in heaps or in the barnyard. Such manure, when applied in the spring, makes dry soil still dryer, and unless plowed well down where it will do the young plants little or no good, it would burn them up if the season should be hot and dry.

By plowing time in the spring this manure will have become thoroughly mixed with the soil and will be worked through the soil, thus affording an abundance of plant food in all stages of growth. Manure is the food of all plants, and you must afford an abundance of available plant food if you expect good returns from your vegetable or fruit garden. Garden soil sometimes becomes surfeited with stable manure. In this case cover with lime, use commercial fertilizer, or plow under a crop of clover or other soiling crop.

Unfortunate is the gardener who fails to see the adaptability of his soil which must in a certain degree decide the value of the crop he grows. A poorly adapted soil is a great drawback to successful gardening.

Preparing the Soil.

The time of plowing varies to meet the requirements of different soils, seasons and localities; and every piece must be considered by itself. Means should be taken for starting the plow as soon as circumstances permit.

In dry soils and well drained localities the plow can be used much earlier than on heavy soils. Nothing is gained by plowing heavy soils until they are in a proper condition, but rather the reverse, for they will become lumpy and it will be late in the season before the lumps can be pulverized and brought into a condition to impart nutriment to the growing crops.

If the plowing has been left till spring such soils should be plowed when in that condition of moisture to insure mellowness and fine tilth. To determine when soil is in the the right condition for plowing or cultivating, take a portion in the hand; if it packs and sticks to your fingers it is too wet, while if it crushes hard it is too dry. In both cases it will be hard and lumpy, and will take a long time to bring it to the condition necessary for good results.

A loose, well pulverized soil allows the air to circulate freely among its particles, and the spreading roots of the plants reach out and draw their sustenance from a more extended surface than in soils which have assumed a compact form. Seeds sown on a compact soil cannot be expected to produce other than a sickly growth of plants. It should be borne in mind that a good crop on one acre is better than half a crop on two acres. The production of crops is not a matter of chance as many may suppose, but depends on the care bestowed upon them. While it may not be possible to choose such soil as is desired, much may be done in the way of artificial improvement by draining, manuring, etc.

The soil should be well drained unless of such a nature as to render this unnecessary. Muck, manure and other fertilizers should be abundantly used. A sandy loam is one of the best soils we have, being rich in vegetable matter. Alluvial soils are well adapted to vegetables but not to small fruits. One of the best soils we have is a rich, gravelly loam. Such soil retains moisture longer than a sandy soil and is adapted to the growth of a greater variety of crops than any other and when mixed with vegetable matter is one of our most valuable soils.

Another point of importance is the fining and compacting of the soil as soon as plowed in hot, dry weather. In preparing soil for garden crops during summer it is best not to wait to do a whole day's plowing, but every few hours to pulverize what has been plowed, and for this purpose there is nothing better than the plank drag. Evaporation is so rapid in the hot summer days that land will often dry out in a single day so that a good seed bed cannot be formed unless the soil is pulverized immediately after plowing.

Tools.

Although not really necessary, it is of great advantage to

have an assortment of tools for thoroughly preparing the soil, and to facilitate the labor of caring for the crop and destroying weeds and insects.

Where the garden is cared for as it should be there will be little or no chance for the weeds to start. While there is generally an assortment of tools on every farm suitable for use in the garden, I will give a list of those adapted to garden use.

First is the Plow. For breaking the ground in spring use a common two-horse plow. This puts the manure down as desired and takes a generous slice at each cross. So long as the fresh manure does not come in direct contact with the plants it will be hardly possible to put on too much, but it is best to use nothing but thoroughly decayed manure. It is also best to cut a narrow furrow when plowing, as then the manure becomes more thoroughly incorporated with the soil. Always keep your tools bright, sharp and clean, as it is much easier to use a bright, sharp hoe or plow; then too, the work is done in a much better style than where dull, rusty tools are used. And, it will go to show that you too are also sharp and bright.

Next to the plow comes the Harrow, which should also be sharp; it is then a splendid tool for making a fine seed bed on which to sow seeds, or for setting out small plants. Where more land has been broken than is needed for immediate planting, it is a good plan to run over it with the harrow, keeping it clean and in good condition for planting, as you can take advantage of a shower to set out cabbage, tomato, celery and other plants while the soil is wet. Commence planting when, or just before, the rain begins so that the plants will receive the benefit of the shower.

Next comes the Roller, which is very handy for pulverizing the soil when hard and lumpy. A small hand roller about three feet long is very convenient for rolling in small seeds when sown by hand. The value of compacting the soil about freshly sown seed, especially in summer, cannot be over-estimated.

The Wheel Hoe is a very convenient tool in the caring for crops and should be one of the best obtainable. A good implement does not throw the dirt over small plants, and the rows can be worked closely, so that it is unnecessary to go over the rows with a hand hoe after the plants have been thinned. Keep all cutting parts bright and sharp. To obtain the best results with this tool you should go over each row two or three times so as to work the soil over thoroughly. When kept sharp and bright it will surprise you to note how easy it is to run one, and how much better work is done; and a man can hoe an acre a day when the soil is in good condition.

A Seed Drill is a very convenient implement, but is quite expensive and not practical in the garden when we consider that it is not often that there are more than one or two rows sown to any one kind of seed, and this can be done in almost the time it would take to set the drill. The combined drill and hoe is a delusion and a snare. Don't experiment. If you want a satisfactory tool *don't have any combinations about it.*

And, too, you will need a good strong garden line, long enough to reach across the garden. This will be very useful to assist in laying out the garden neatly. A good line well cared for will last for years, and will be one of the requisites for the garden as there must be no hit or miss work if you expect to succeed, as every plant must be in the row. Where it is necessary to keep a few inches from the row to avoid cutting the plants that are out of the row, either the soil will not be worked up to the row as it should be, or has to be gone over with the hand hoe, which consumes considerable time where much ground is under cultivation.

The Hand Hoe. This tool is so well known and universally used as to need no directions as to its use. It should be kept sharp and bright, however, as it will then not only be much easier to use but will also do much better work. When sharpening a hoe, grind or file on the front instead of the back. It will then slip into the soil much easier.

The Steel Rake. There is no tool of more real value in the garden when kept well in use than the steel rake. The benefit is three-fold. Pulverizing the soil for an inch or two in depth prevents the escape of moisture from below, increases the growth of plants and destroys the weeds before they can make an appearance. The mistake of supposing that stirring the soil is not necessary unless there is a visable sign of growth of weeds to be destroyed should be abandoned. The surface should not only be kept clean, but frequently broken up and mellow. The pulverization of the soil should be kept near the surface not only to insure safety to the roots of the plants, but because the moisture in the soil is retained better than by deeper mellowing. The rake also enables the laborer to work much faster than with the hoe, and if used as often as it should be will pass over the ground with remarkable ease. (When through using the rake or hoe hang them up, for they are dangerous things to step on). The space between the rows of cabbage, beans, peas, celery, etc., may thus be kept clean with little labor.

Garden Trowels, Spades, etc., are also very useful in the

garden and must have care, and an occasional call on the grindstone.

Laying Out the Garden.

As before stated, a parallelogram is the best shape for a kitchen garden, as it renders more easy the preparation of the soil, and also the cultivation of the crops. On the outside next the boundaries a border of about ten feet should be left for the growing of the smaller vegetables, which should be sown in beds; those on the sunny side for the early ones and those on the northernly side that require shade. The rows (for the seeds in these beds should never be sown broadcast), should run with the slope of the land wherever possible and should be the long way of the plot.

In winter while there is plenty of time before spring work comes on, the year's work should be planned; what varieties to plant, the quantities of each required, in what part of the garden to plant each variety so as to avoid the crossing of the different species, etc., and thereby spoiling each other. Then, too, if the soil is of different quality in different parts of the garden, it should be planned so that the heavy and light soils shall be occupied by such crops as best succeed on the respective soils. Ease of cultivation and the rotation of crops should also be brought into consideration. The smaller varieties which require hoeing should be together; also those that mature at the same time, and those that require horse culture, making it much easier to prepare the soil for the succeeding or second crop. When laying out a new garden, when it comes to the second season, rotation should be especially considered, as no two crops of the same varieties should be raised on the same ground two succeeding seasons as each consumes certain properties of plant food from the soil, so this change must be made so that the soil may be kept in a good state of cultivation.

Reference must also be made to the kind of food each plant requires, as for instance, potatoes and strawberries should not succeed each other, as each requires considerable potash for their development; therefore does it not stand to reason that where the soil has produced a crop of one it would of necessity develop but a small crop of the other if planted in close succession, if the deficiency has not been supplied? Neither should cabbage follow oats in direct succession, as the latter seems to poison the soil for the growth of the former.

It is much cheaper to work the garden with the plow than with the spade, so where sufficient land is to be had a large garden is much better, and can be cared for proportionately much cheaper, than a small one, and your supply of potatoes, sugar corn, squashes, melons, as well as smaller vegetables can be had in profusion. In planting, sow a variety of seeds so that the different tastes may be supplied; not only your own, but other people's as well.

No fruit trees of any description should be allowed to grow in the kitchen garden, as they are a source of continual annoyance, while in time their spreading roots and tops render them a nuisance. They not only injure the vegetables, but they themselves are injured by plow and spade. Fruit trees should be planted separately where they may receive proper attention and not be an impediment to the care of the garden.

It is of great importance to rapid work and good gardening that all these points should be arranged in the mind, or on paper, before work begins in the spring. The plan, if kept, would be quite beneficial to the operator the following season as it indicates where each variety was grown the season before.

Compost.

Every gardener should have a generous supply of this, as it is greatly superior to coarse manure for garden use, especially in making hills for melons, cucumbers, tomatoes, sweet potatoes, in celery trenches, etc. It should be stacked in the autumn and thoroughly decomposed.

It is composed of hen manure, hog manure, barnyard scrapings, ashes, leaves, bean and pea vines, or green weeds; in fact anything that will decay and make fertilizer, of which you really cannot have too much. If made in the fall, as recommended, so much the better, as it will then become thoroughly decayed before needed; but it must not be exposed to the weather, as this will cause it to leach out and much of its value to be lost. To prevent this it may be covered with old boards, or may be in some out building. Fork over occasionally to prevent burning and promote decay, always keeping the heaps flat on top, and moist by giving it a soaking whenever possible with washing suds, liquid manure, etc.

To make a good compost the heap should be one-half soil or ashes. Night soil may also be made into a valuable fertilizer by putting it into the compost heap or by mixing with soil or coal ashes. You really cannot make too much manure on the farm.

Manure.

It is a good thing to make manure and a better thing to save it. Manure is the food of plants, and you cannot expect good returns from your garden or fields unless the crops are supplied with nourishment. Therefore a good supply should either be made or otherwise procured, as the garden should have a heavy dressing at least two years out of three.

The supply may be largely increased by pulling the cabbage stumps, pea vines, or other refuse, as fast as the crops are gathered, and throwing on the manure heap. This should be near the house so that the ashes and slops may be thrown upon it to increase the amount and promote decay. Where tall weeds, corn stalks, etc., are thrown upon the heap it should be forked over whenever possible, as this will prevent burning and loss, and will greatly facilitate rotting and handling when needed; besides, they will not interfere with the cultivation of small plants as they would otherwise do.

Barnyard manure well cared for contains all the plant food elements required by plants. It not only brings permanent fertility to the soil with the potash, nitrogen and phosphoric acid which it contains, but it renders the stored up materials more available, improves the condition of the soil, makes it warmer, and enables it to retain the moisture. Poultry droppings are very valuable.

It may be composted with muck, leaves (these are also very valuable), or other absorbents kept dry and stored in barrels and used in the hill. Never mix with ashes or the ammonia which it contains will be lost. Do not allow it to heat. It may be dissolved in water and used in watering plants, when its value will be quickly seen.

Garden soil sometimes becomes surfeited with manure. In this case use phosphate, lime, or sow part at least to clover or rye, which when plowed under will supply plant food in another form. When plowed, broadcast lime on the surface, giving it a good dressing. Lime and phosphate should not be used the same season as the lime will destroy the phosphate, thereby incurring loss.

In applying manure to land, care should be taken to spread it evenly, breaking the lumps to pieces. However, this should not be done long before plowing, especially if the weather be hot, dry or windy, for if it is, the manure will dry, its properties evaporate, and loss accrue. The custom practiced by some of piling the manure in small heaps all over the ground is a bad one, as the heavy spring rains wash the valuable qualities into the ground under the heap, while the soil between the heaps does not receive the least benefit therefrom; then, too, the soil under the heaps will be wet and soggy until late in the season. By all means spread it as fast as drawn from the pile. Another way and one which I prefer, is to plow the land and spread the manure, and then harrow it in. In this case the manure must be very fine. Where it is coarse the former is the best way.

The most valuable elements of manure cannot be measured by the cord or ton, as they are the liquid and gaseous elements, which are the most difficult to retain. They are the first to escape, and escape unnoticed through such an easy outlet.

Fertilizers.

There is no doubt that a great deal of these are wasted by many who use them; wasted, not because the soil does not need them, but for want of proper knowledge of how to apply them and the special fertilizer required for the particular soils, plants, etc. Different soils do not require the same kind of dressing, and expensive experiments may be made in different localities, while so confused will be the result that they will prove of little or no value.

First, we must learn what the soil needs before we know what to apply; second, we must know what each plant requires before we can fertilize intelligently. Hit or miss experiments prove nothing and are useless. It is important to go at anything intelligently or failure may result, and none are more likely to fail than the tiller of the soil. Before using chemical manure he must learn that one soil is rich in potash, another in nitrogen, another in phosphoric acid, and another in lime; to apply any of these to soils where there is already an abundance, will only be a loss to the owner.

We must begin our studies of fertilizers and soil requirements at the bottom, and then our progress will be rapid, because our work will be intelligently done. In using commercial fertilizers it is best to sow them between the rows and then work them around the plants during the season with the cultivator or hoe.

Procuring Supplies—Seeds, Plants, Etc.

During the winter evenings it is a good idea to look over your stock of seeds and make out a list of your requirements for the coming season. Take your wife into the scheme with you, and procure seeds to secure a variety to cover the entire season, flower as well as vegetable; but do not entertain the idea that you need the contents of a seed and plant establishment, for this is a mistake. A few varieties are best.

Having the season's campaign all settled, the next thing is to know what is to be grown, the varieties best adapted to the locality and the soil of your garden, and where to obtain them of the best quality. If you have saved them yourself you are comparatively safe, but if they were purchased they should not be used until thoroughly tested unless you know they came from a trustworthy source. It does not pay to try to economize in the purchase of seeds, nor does it pay to use poor seeds on any part of the farm, as it is a waste of time, labor, ground, manure and patience, as the inferior vegetables will scarcely cover expenses, for nowhere on the farm is "blooded stock" of more importance than in the seeds sown.

In making out your order stick to the varieties known to be good and that suit your soil and local climate, especially if grown for private use, for the greatest pleasure is derived from testing the fruits of your own raising with the appetite engendered through their cultivation. In some cases I think it best to purchase your supply of seed and plants from a reliable dealer who has his reputation at stake and who will fill your order with nothing but the best.

Then, it is not advisable to try all the novelties you see offered in gaudy colors and glowing terms, for general use, but rather buy those that you know to be good and suited to your requirements. Many of the novelties are not suited to all climates and while they may do well in one locality they may from one reason or another be worthless in another. This rule also applies to older varieties. For this reason we will not name any particular varieties, but will leave this to the choice of the gardener. Then, too, many novelties are new only in name; this is a fraud practiced by some seedsmen. In selecting, choose those varieties that do well for your neighbors, while if you desire, include a few novelties for trial, but do not depend on them for a main crop until you have given them a fair trial, or disappointment may follow. It is a very interesting matter to test a few of them, watching their growth, testing their quality, etc., and there is occasionally some money to be made through their culture, but don't go in too deep.

Raising Plants.

With a garden of an acre or so it will be found economical to raise your own supply of plants. For this you will need hot beds, cold frames and beds of rich fine soil, if it is properly done. It is best to locate these in a sunny nook where they will be sheltered from the cold winds and also near the cistern and manure pile. These beds must be well drained as dampness is very injurious to young seedlings, and will also take up a considerable amount of heat, which should go to the forwarding of the plants.

It is advisable to sift the soil through a coarse sieve as it then makes a fine seed bed for the young plants. As soon as the temperature has fallen to 75°, or as soon as the soil is only just warm to palm of the hand, the soil should be sprinkled and when it has dried off a little it should be raked thoroughly and the seeds sown.

I prefer sowing in drills as much stockier plants will thus be secured. The drills should be about four inches apart; this will allow light and air to reach the roots and will permit of an occasional cultivation. Seeds will not grow if placed too deeply in the soil. Some seeds like cabbage, brusselsprouts, etc., should be about one-half an inch deep, while smaller seeds like celery should be simply pressed into the soil. A good rule is to cover the seeds about five or six times the diameter of the seed. A light covering firmly pressed down is all that is required.

About ten weeks before the last frost is expected is about the time to sow seeds of tender plants, while eight weeks will answer for the hardier varieties. The plants will then be ready for the warm days and showers of spring. The plants in the beds should be aired on every warm day that they may not become "drawn" and spindling. They should not be allowed to crowd each other in the beds, but should be thinned freely or they will be severely damaged.

Another point to be remembered and that is, to not keep the soil too damp or the plants will damp off. Water only when the soil is dry on top. If you are troubled with the little white worms in the soil of your plant beds try soot water, tobacco tea, lime water, or water with hard water. The last is the best remedy I am acquainted with. As planting time approaches the beds should be left open, whenever possible, that they may become sufficiently hardened so as not to miss the covering when removed to the open air.

Where a few extra early plants are wanted they can be removed to the earliest beds when the cabbage or other hardy plants have been set out, and the sash put on again. While the hardy plants may be set out as soon as danger of frost is past, the tender plants such as tomato, egg and pepper plants should not be set out until the thermometer stands at sixty degrees all night, or when the swallows begin housekeeping. Good thrifty plants well hardened before transplanting are necessary for a good crop.

Seeds for reasonably early plants may be sown in cold frames in the same manner as in the hot bed. These will not have the advantage of the heat caused by the fermenting manure, depending solely on the heat of the sun and the protection afforded by the sash for their development. They should be sown about two weeks later than when the hot bed is used, and the plants will be ready for transplanting two weeks later than those raised in heat. As soon as warm enough to dig and bring them into a fine condition seed beds should be made in a warm, sunny nook in the garden, for the sowing of late cabbage, cauliflower, celery, etc. Where no beds are at hand or where only a few plants are required, they can be grown quite satisfactorily in boxes set in a sunny window in a warm room.

For this purpose some boxes (tobacco boxes are nice for this) should be procured, and filled with some fine rich soil; after the seeds are sown keep them warm and moist, *not* wet. Do not allow the plants to become crowded. Transplanting the young seedlings at least once, is quite essential to their proper development. This should be done before they become crowded in the seed bed. They should be set far enough apart to allow them to attain some growth and make them stocky. Care should be taken not to bruise the plants or break the roots. To prevent this, handle carefully. Moistening the soil before removing the plants will be of assistance to you in preventing this. In removing plants to the open ground this is quite essential.

Before going into other details it will be well to say a few words about

Watering and Transplanting.

The most suitable time for transplanting is in the afternoon or evening or on a rainy day. But if done on a hot, dry day, water thoroughly and shade for two or three days. New roots will have now formed and all danger from transplanting is past. Nature never intended for a plant to be transplanted and care must be exercised in so doing.

Don't crowd the roots into a hole not half large enough to receive them, but make the hole large and deep enough to hold the roots with the soil adhering to them. Make the soil fine and mellow, and the hills large. With one hand place the plant in position in the hole, while with the other pour water into the hole. If properly done the mellow soil will fill in about the roots and hold the plant in position, so that, if freshly taken from the bed it will scarcely ever wilt, even if transplanted in hot sunshine. When the water has settled away, fill around the plant with mellow soil. If treated in this way the soil will not bake around the plant as it would otherwise do. Never pour water on or around newly set plants, for it is almost sure to cause the soil to bake or the sun to scald and injure them. As soon as they have become established, loosen the soil around their stems, always keeping the soil loose, clean and mellow. If a little hen manure is worked into the soil around the plants, it will greatly increase the growth as well as the productiveness of the plants.

In regard to watering the garden, I would say that more harm than good results come from beginning to water a plant and then not keeping it up till the necessity ceases. As soon as the soil dries out after watering it should be stirred with a hoe. *Water thoroughly or do not water at all.* Then, too, it is not natural for a plant to receive water while the sun is shining. Therefore do not sprinkle the foliage or damages will result. Water on cloudy days or in the evening. Instead of watering (and this takes considerable time and labor), I prefer to keep the soil loose and mellow around the roots. For this purpose there is nothing better than the steel rake before mentioned. This not only fills the place of watering, through evaporation of the moisture from below, but serves to keep the soil free from weeds and in good condition for the succeeding crop, where two crops are grown on same ground in one season; and it is much easier done.

Saving Seed.

When saving seed of vegetables as in any other crop the very best should be selected. The best heads of lettuce, the best beets, cabbage, ears of corn; in fact the best of everything.

Care must also be exercised to keep each variety pure, as crossing with other varieties is ofttimes detrimental to quality. All seed must be well cleansed, cured, labeled, dated, and put away where there is no danger from freezing, mice, dampness or very warm heat.

By continual selection in one direction a strain is established that is perhaps better suited to your locality than any you can buy, while some varieties such as peas, beans, potatoes, etc., are best when procured from the north. Where the runts of crops are saved for seed year after year, the quality of the seeds will deteriorate and the crop will not pay expenses and "gardening don't pay." From this reason we so often hear the complaint, "my lettuce isn't fit to eat; my cabbage don't head; my sweetcorn has lost its flavor." All these and other complaints too numerous to mention are heard from the discouraged and disappointed gardener. In selecting seeds always keep a point in view.

Hot Beds.

These are very valuable appliances to the gardener's outfit whether he gardens for market or for his own private use. All plants that require starting in heat may be sown in the hot bed. An ordinary sash is three by six feet. Allowing a slant of 6 inches from back to front the width of the frame is easily calculated. A good bed (and no other should be made), must be at least 3 feet 6 inches deep and well drained. For material 2 inch stuff for corner posts and good inch boards for sides.

Cedar or cypress boards are best as they last longer. Make the rear posts 3 feet 6 inches long and the front ones 36 inches. After nailing all together let the

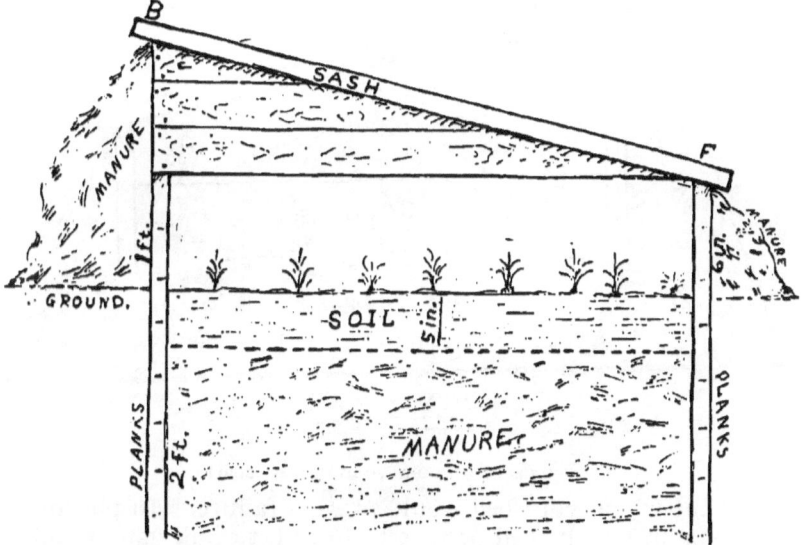

End view of Hot Bed showing interior.

frame down 2 feet 6 inches into the earth, facing the south so as to catch the rays of the sun. Where several sashes are to be used the posts should be set firmly in the ground. Where seeds of tender plants and hardy ones are to be sown in the same frame, or a portion of it used as a cold frame, a partition must be placed across the frame so as to give the separate parts proper treatment. Where the sashes meet, 2x3 inch strips should be nailed across the bed for the sash to rest on and an inch strip placed down the center of this scantling to keep the sash in place when moved back and forth.

If a warm day or two comes in January or February the pit may be dug out 2 feet 6 in. deep, the frame put in place, manure banked against it, and leaves or litter put in to keep out the frost. Care must be exercised in the construction of the bed as your future success depends on this. The sash should fit the frame closely and the glass should have one-quarter inch lap—shingle fashion. In preparing the manure use horse manure (hen manure will do but is not so reliable), not more than six weeks old, containing considerable straw or leaves.

This should be forked over and if dry, watered and allowed to stand a few days to heat, then it should be forked over again, when it will be ready for use in a few days. The reason for forking it over is to obtain a uniform heat

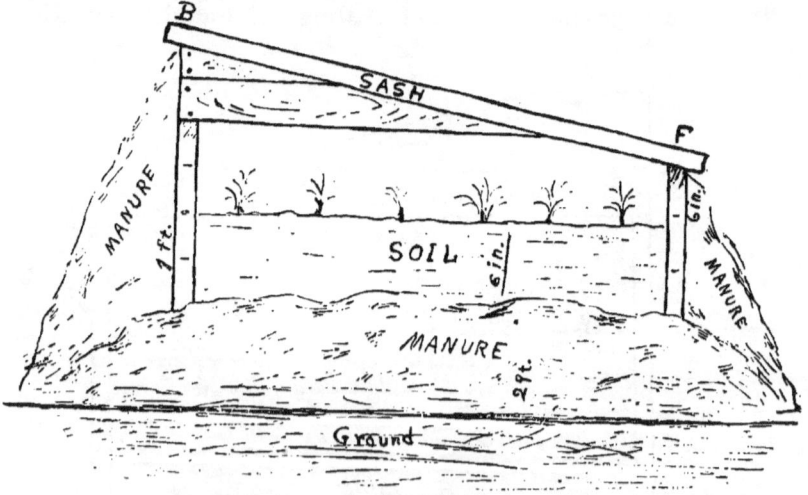

This style is recommended for a wet location.

without which your bed would prove a failure. In placing the manure in the bed be sure to spread it evenly and tread it down firmly. This is of great importance and unless done one portion of the bed will heat more quickly than the other, causing the soil to settle unevenly. The soil used for the bed should be dry and a rich sandy loam. After the bed is complete put on the sash and bank up with manure.

Do not sow your seed until the temperature is about 75° or 80°, at which point it should be kept. One point of importance is, that you use dry soil in making your hot bed, and that the first heat shall pass off before sowing the seed, otherwise your seed and labor will be lost and your hot bed prove a failure. Be very careful about the temperature, keeping it even and moist as possible and not too high—never over 85°. It is advisable to keep a thermometer in the bed at all times when in use. The hot bed should not be idle but should be occupied throughout the entire spring and early summer. A spent hot bed affords an admirable place for storing celery in the winter. A good hot bed sash and frame well painted and cared for will last for years.

Soil for hot beds may be shoveled into the old bed and covered with leaves and the shutters or old boards laid over all. This keeps hard frosts out and permits the soil to be worked early in the spring.

The Cold Frame.

The cold frame is a valuable appliance in the spring and is simply a hot bed minus the heating material. The frame may be of any size from one to four sash. Each sash should be 3x6 feet, the same as for hot beds previously mentioned. The frame should be 16 inches high in front and 2 feet high in rear, and should be constructed of inch and a half plank. Cedar or cypress is best for this purpose on account of their durability.

When two or more sash are used, braces four inches wide must be placed across the frame from back to front to hold the sash in position and strengthen the frame. On these braces a strip must be nailed to separate the sash and cause them to run true. On each side or end of the frame a strip projecting above the ends the thickness of the sash must be nailed to keep the sash in place.

When completed set upon the ground, in a sheltered place, and bank up with manure to keep out the frost as much as possible. This should be done in March, and as soon as the weather will permit, or as soon as there is no danger of freezing in the frame, the plants may be transplanted to it from the hot bed. In this way they become stocky and well rooted, and when ready to be set in the open garden can be moved without scarcely feeling the change. This is the place, too, to forward tomato, pepper and egg plants. Here also many seeds may be sown and bulbs started before set in the ground. Cauliflower, celery and cabbage plants may be brought along to advantage in the cold frame. Here is also a good place to store celery in the winter, but must be protected with litter to exclude frost.

The cold frame, like the hot bed, must be thoroughly drained. Seeds should be sown in the hot bed about ten weeks before the last frost is expected, or in this latitude early in March. By the first of April the plants will be large enough to be pricked out into the cold frame, and then shaded when the sun is warm, and watered. If the plants are set in shallow boxes when moved to the frame they will be easier to care for. They should be kept as warm as possible while in the frames, but must be well aired in the middle of warm, sunny days. A few melons, cucumbers, squashes, lima beans, etc., may be planted in the cold frame in sods or otherwise, and when the weather has become settled they may be moved to the open ground. They may thus be brought into bearing several days before the regular crop is ready.

Those who have a cold frame but no hot bed, can procure plants from a hot bed and care for them in the cold frame and thus have their supply when actually needed.

What to Grow and How to Grow It.

We will now endeavor to tell what to grow and how it is to be grown, to the best advantage, so far as our knowledge is concerned. Of course a great deal depends on the skill and experience of the gardener, and on local conditions and circumstances which no one can foresee and over which we have no control.

We have also placed the cultural directions alphabetically, so as to give this treatise a more systematical appearance, and to render more easy the finding of any particular subject which you may have in mind. In consideration of this we will first give the instruction on the culture of the

Artichoke (*Synara Scolymus*).—This is the French variety, the flower buds of which are so highly esteemed as an article of food and is entirely different from those cultivated for its roots or tubers. Artichokes require good deep soil somewhat moist, and if of a sandy nature so much more in their favor. Seed may be sown in the hot bed or cold frame and removed into pots, so as to give plenty of room and air until danger from frost is past, and then transplanted into very rich soil two feet apart each way. Or the plants may be raised in beds outside, but in that case they will not be likely to bear the first season. In raising them in this way the seed should be sown in rows one foot apart early in spring. When the seedlings have attained sufficient growth they should be transplanted to their permanent home. The edible portion is the flower heads while in an undeveloped state, which will be produced from September until killed by frost.

Before planting the soil should be made very rich with well decayed manure. After planting water freely and keep the weeds in check. Late in the fall, before severe weather, cut off the tops and cover the crowns with leaves or litter to protect from frost. The second year the heads will commence to form about July. Where blanched artichokes are desired, they can be obtained by cutting back the stems in July close to the surface, when the young and fast growing shoots which grow up after cutting may be blanched similar to celery.

The undeveloped buds are cooked like asparagus. On account of its hardiness, easy cultivation and perennial nature it should be found in every garden.

Plant the tubers of the Jerusalem variety like potatoes, and sufficient is usually left in the soil to seed the ground for the next season. As they do not yield satisfactory after three or more years, it is best to make a new bed every four years at most. To destroy the plants, plow the ground when they are about a foot in height; at this time the old tubers have rotted and the new crop not yet formed.

We think the Artichoke is far too little grown, which is the case with many other vegetables. The tuberous variety is a great hog food when grown on a large scale, as they are a cheap, healthy and nutritious diet on which hogs thrive most splendidly.

Asparagus (*Asparagus Officinalis*).—This delicious vegetable like many others is too little grown and but few people, comparatively speaking, know how delicious it really is, while it is also one of the first to appear.

The seed should be sown in drills one foot apart and one inch in depth. Before sowing pour boiling water on the seed and pour off immediately. This assists in sprouting the seed without injuring it, if done quickly. Care must be taken to keep down all weeds the first season as soon as they appear or they will choke out the young seedlings. The deeper the soil and the more manure used, the greater will be the crop.

The soil best suited to the growth of Asparagus is a rich loam inclining to be light, and the manure must be well rotted. The most economical width for an asparagus bed is five feet, which will take three rows, one down the center and one down each side about a foot from the edge. Transplant to their permanent home when growth begins in the spring. This operation cannot be done too carefully. Set the plants not less than fifteen inches apart in the rows; lay the roots out regularly and neatly and about four inches in depth. The permanent beds should be prepared by stirring the soil deeply and should be thoroughly enriched. Where the subsoil is not naturally loose and mellow it should be made so by plowing or otherwise.

After the plants are well rooted give frequent and thorough cultivation, drawing more soil up to the plants each time. The after cultivation consists simply in keeping the ground clean, and in dressing with manure, salt and ashes in spring. Early the following spring spade in a heavy coat of manure and a quart of salt to the square rod, and cultivate until the plants begin to die. The third season the bed may be cut over two or three times, cutting all the shoots no matter how small, and after the last cutting give the bed a dressing as before.

The next season, as well as all following ones, the bed should give a full crop and should be given an annual dressing as before, and should be well, but not deeply, cultivated until the plants occupy the whole space. As soon as the tops ripen they should be cut and burned. Asparagus may also be set in the autumn if the bed is well drained so as to prevent water standing on it. It is a good plan to protect the beds with strawy manure or litter, which may be burned off in early spring before plants appear. Or if this covering is worked into the soil, you will soon have a supply of this most delicious vegetable. The young shoots may be cut for use the second season, but not very freely until the third, as before stated.

After the bed has become thoroughly established very little attention is required except keeping the soil clean and well dressed. For this reason it pays to make a good bed. Asparagus is a marine plant and requires more or less salt. It is also an old favorite, and was grown to perfection 200 years before the Christian era. If prompt returns are wanted it is best to purchase good two-year-old plants; for in sowing the seed the "grass" will not be ready for use until at least a year later.

In selecting a location regards should be had to the preparation of the remainder of the garden. All permanent beds and plantations should be together on one side of the plot. So far as possible the soil should be plowed deeply and heavily manured, for this is one of those plants that it is difficult to make the soil too rich for. Give the plants plenty of sun. Shading them too much is a mistake too often made. The distance given in setting the plants is the limit; a trifle farther apart is still better. It is not necessary to set the plants very deeply—four inches is sufficient, as the roots spread out and grow. See that the soil is pressed firmly around the plants when set out.

Asparagus will thrive in almost any soil, but a light, rich loam is best and will produce a crop earlier than a clay soil. The best place for early potatoes is the best for asparagus. The deeper and richer the soil the better, but the idea that soil must be deeply trenched, and an extraordinary amount of manure applied is now out of date. A southern slope near the farm building is a splendid place for asparagus. Do not plant on gravelly soil.

The commercial fertilizer best suited to this crop is 1000 pounds of raw bone, and 200 pounds of muriate of potash per acre. In case it rains soon after planting, rake the surface carefully to destroy the weeds and to keep the soil mellow. In doing this, care should be exercised to avoid injuring the tender shoots which may have started. Cultivate quite frequently. Do this as early as possible, for the earlier the soil is stirred and the air let in, the earlier the "grass" will be ready for use. The natural tendency of the crowns is to grow near the surface; therefore care must taken to cultivate very shallow near the rows.

After cutting the stalks the bed should be forced to do its best. This is done by covering the bed with fine manure or compost, and as soon as cutting ceases and when the stalks have grown again, work the manure into the soil. This gives the plants new vigor and strength to produce a good crop the coming season. A little salt sown on the bed in the spring will assist in keeping down the weeds, stimulate the "grass," dissolve the plant food in the manure and attract moisture. In cutting it is best to cut even with, or a little below, the surface, using a pointed knife, which is less liable to injure the unseen sprouts. Every shoot however small should be cut, for the good of the next season's crop. If the asparagus beetle puts in an appearance, prompt actions on your part are necessary. If a few broods of young chicks or turkeys are allowed to inspect the patch a great many of the pests will be destroyed. If the old tops are cut and burned in the autumn millions of eggs will be destroyed.

Beans (*Faba*).—Every garden should have a good supply of these general favorites in it, as there is scarcely a person who does not enjoy them, either green or dry, while they have a history long and curious. Pliny says of them, "The pod is to be eaten with the seed." From this we conclude he was speaking of what we know as "string beans." We also find them recorded in 2d Samuel XVII, 28, and also in Ezekiel IV, 9. Beans are divided into two classes—dwarf and pole, and these subdivided into green podded and wax podded.

BEANS (*Faba Vulgaris*). No crop responds to good treatment more readily than this. F. Vulgaris is the common garden variety. A succession of plantings may be made from May throughout the summer in rows 18 to 36 inches apart; in hills two inches deep, one foot apart, and three seeds to a hill. A deeply tilled light, rich soil is best suited to their growth. Being tender and very susceptible to cold they must not be planted too early. That soil which was manured for a previous crop is best suited to their growth. For an extra early supply a few may be sown in the cold frame, and when the weather is settled they may be transplanted to the garden when about three inches high.

The snap varieties yield very abundantly and a drill of 75 to 100 feet in length will produce sufficient to meet the requirements of an average family, for if they are picked closely, as they should be, the plants will continue to bear for a considerable length of time. The pole variety will commence to bear about the time the dwarfs cease and are sometimes preferred from the fact that they are more productive, and are more easily harvested.

In selecting varieties care should be taken to select only those that are stringless, as they are much easier to prepare for use and are much more tender when cooked. Cultivate thoroughly and draw the soil up to their stems twice during growth. Never cultivate when wet, nor when in bloom, as this will greatly injure them.

POLE BEANS (*Phaseolus multiflorus*). No garden, however small, is complete unless it contains a generous supply of these real luxuries. Yet the work of poling them and keeping them trained is frequently such a perplexing one that they are often entirely discarded.

They may be planted in hills 36 inches apart, but must not be put in the ground until the middle of May, or when the swallows begin to nest, or when the trees are in full leaf. The poles should not be more than 6 feet high when set, or it will be inconvenient to gather the crop when ready for use; and, too, the vines will not begin to bear until they have reached the tops of the poles. If any fail to climb the poles readily they should be twined around the poles, in the same direction as the others, or they will not take to the poles readily, if at all. Pinching out the tips of the vines tends to produce an earlier supply, but in my opinion diminishes the crop. It does not take long to secure a good supply of poles, and when once secured it is not much trouble to preserve them for a number of years. If kept out of doors they should be stacked, tops downward. To prevent the ends from rotting off they should be charred slightly, or dipped in coal tar, which will preserve them for years.

The poles should be set by the aid of the garden line, and the crooked ones turned into the row; this will give them a neater appearance. Then put some compost around each one, working it into the soil. Three or four beans may be planted around each pole, when the vines will cover them in a short time and will present a beautiful sight, heavily laden with their long handsome pods.

Some varieties do well when planted in the hills of corn. In this case the variety should be of a loosely twining nature. The pods should be picked while young and tender when required for string beans, and by taking care to gather the older pods, the blooming and bearing will continue for a lengthened period. These are even more susceptible to cold and to hot winds than are the dwarf varieties; and where the hills are to be the soil should be raised as for melons. It is said that by setting the poles at an angle of $35°$, the tops to the north, the vines will bear earlier, the pods be straighter, and more easily gathered. As the matured beans or pods are all that is used, the season in the north is too short for a succession; then, too, this is unnecessary for when the directions are observed a few poles will bear throughout the season. Of the "snaps," the "wax" varieties are the best, being the most tender, while they are of the most superb quality.

The KIDNEY or FRENCH BEAN (*Phaseolus nanus*) is another division of the common garden bean, which is very tender and must have warm dry soil to succeed. They are cultivated similar to the common varieties.

LIMAS. The principal point in the culture of these real delicacies is to get them started properly. This class of beans is really more liable to decay in the ground than the common varieties unless the soil is warm and dry. Therefore it is best to plant in a hill, slightly raised above the level with a shovelful of light manure or compost in the hills, which should be three feet apart.

These also require poles to ramble over, similar to the pole beans. The Bush Limas are a great acquisition where poles are hard to procure, but having the poles I prefer the old Pole Lima, for various reasons. In planting Lima beans be very careful to place the eye of the bean downward as the first leaves (which is the bean itself) are quite large and heavy; it will assist them in coming up if planted in this manner. Cover very lightly with very fine light soil, sand or chaff, being very careful not to plant until the soil is warm and light. Corn planting time is a good time to plant Lima beans.

When the frost kills the vines in the fall, gather the green beans and dry them for winter use. They then taste like fresh beans. Three plants to a pole is sufficient. Every garden should have a supply of this delectable bean.

Beet (*Beta vulgaris*).—This is another universal favorite. The beet is a half-hardy biennial and like all other root crops produces best results in a rich, sandy loam, which has been well manured for a previous crop, otherwise forked or illshaped roots may result. For an early supply the seed should be sown in the hot bed, and the outside leaves cut off when transplanted to the open ground.

Where the proper soil is not at your disposal, the soil should be dug before winter and a dressing of manure applied. By this method the soil becomes mellow and pulverized before sowing time. Sow the seed early in April for summer, and in June or July for winter use. Sow in rows 15 to 18 inches apart. It is best to sow in freshly prepared ground, which should be pressed over the seed.

If sown earlier than above, many may run to seed or become coarse and stringy. A few waterings in dry weather will prove beneficial. As soon as the bulbs reach maturity, lift carefully so as not to wound them, pile in heap, cover with sand or earth so as to keep out the frost, and enjoy crisp and tender beets throughout the year. The *blood* beets retain their deep red color when cooked, and present a beautiful appearance when mixed with the yellow fleshed varieties. It will be found advisable to make two or three sowings, so as to be certain of a supply of tender bulbs. Be sure to press the soil firmly about the seed as this is one of the seeds which is slow in germinating. The young plants may be transplanted, but care must be used so as not to injure them, as this will cause them to form misshapen bulbs.

The thinnings of beets when young and tender make an excellent dish when cooked for greens, and are quite profitable where there is a market for them.

The Swiss CHARD is a variety of the common beet grown exclusively for its leaves instead of the bulbs, which are worthless. It is therefore called leaf beet, or spinach beet. After sowing in the spring, the plants are thinned like common beets, and supplied with water. In late summer, autumn and in more southern localities, in early winter, the plants are ready for use.

Beets may be had for winter use by storing in barrels in cellar, and keeping covered with sand or soil to prevent wilting. Beets are on record as a highly prized vegetable over 2000 years ago, and received much notice from early writers on horticultural subjects.

The large rough shells or seed pods contain several seeds making it impossible to sow the seeds thin enough but that they will have to be thinned.

Borecole or Kale (*Brassica oleracea acephala*).—This is another vegetable which is seldom seen in the average vegetable garden. Kale is, practically speaking, a cabbage that does not head, and must be thoroughly cooked. In all the cabbage family this is the most tender and delicate, and would be more generally grown than it is, if its many excellent qualities were more generally known.

Curly GREENS or SCOTCH KALE can accommodate themselves to almost any ordinary garden soil, and no vegetable is more wholesome, coming as it does just after frost has cut off the supply of vegetables, and being hardy may be had throughout the entire winter and spring, by giving protection of straw, leaves, or evergreen boughs, in the north. Sow the seed in May, transplant in June or July, setting the plants in rows two feet apart and one foot between the plants, and give the same culture as recommended for Cabbage.

For a succession sow at intervals of two or three weeks. Seed of the more hardy dwarf varieties may also be sown in the fall and well protected, and should not be transplanted as are the tall varieties. The small heads may be cooked like spinach during winter. The quality is greatly improved by frost and while entirely hardy they should not be handled while frozen. If necessary to handle while in this condition they should be thawed as quickly as possible by immersing them in cold water.

Broccoli (*Brassica oleracea botrytis asparagoides*).—This is nearly related to the cauliflower, but is more hardy, of excellent flavor and greatly relished by all who grow them. Broccoli delights in a good stiff loam.

To maintain a succession care must be given to the sowing at the proper time and to the selecting of the best varieties. The earliest sowings are made in March; the later ones in April or May. The seed is sown in the hot bed or cold frame, the soil being of good depth. Sow thinly and cover lightly with soil. When the plants are three inches high transplant into rows four or five inches apart and the same distance between the plants. If the ground is ready for the setting out of the plants they may be set out in their small state direct from the seed beds, but it is better that they be transplanted once at least.

The permanent plot should be stirred deeply before setting the plants. Some varieties require more space than others, but the medium is about thirty inches each way. After planting give a generous supply of water and also during dry weather an occasional application of liquid manure. Keep the hoe busy during the autumn. On the approach of winter they must be thoroughly protected by a covering of straw or litter, or those which are remaining in the garden will be lost, as the severe winter weather cuts them down unless protection of some kind is given them, and I am doubtful if even this will save them except in favored localities.

The heads should be cut as soon as they attain medium size and cooked similar to the Cauliflower. It may be well to state here that Broccoli and Cauliflower do not thrive in many sections, owing to the fact that the summers are too hot and dry for them, except in favorable localities. The best we can do is to give them a cool, moist situation and risk the crop in unfavorable localities.

Brussels Sprouts (*Brassica oleracea bullata minor*).—This is a superior vegetable, superior to either spinach or kale. It may not be out of place to state here that this, like many other vegetables, is also too little grown.

Sow moderately thick in hot bed in March and thin freely. Prick out into rows four inches apart, on a nicely prepared border, where they will make a stocky growth before they are set out. A plantation should be made from this bed early in May on a good rich soil in rows two feet apart, setting the plants 18 inches apart in the rows. A May sowing should also be made for a late crop, and should be treated in a similar manner.

Look out for the green louse. Hoe frequently, and keep down the weeds. In gathering the sprouts pull those off the stem first, leaving the top till last.

They are cooked and served as are greens. Strip off the outer covering and cook them whole—Ah! what a delicacy, not surpassed by even the Cauliflower. The Sprouts resemble Cabbage in miniature, are produced abundantly, and are about two inches in diameter. They become very tender and of rich delicious flavor when touched by frost.

These like all other members of the *Brassica* family are subject to the ravages of the flea-beetle, the cabbage worm and the green louse. They must be protected against these or they will be severely damaged.

Cabbage (*Brassica oleracea capitata*).—By the introduction of Cabbages of remarkably quick growth it is now possible to obtain a supply of this standard vegetable throughout the year. As to the early history of the Cabbage we will quote the following historical event: Diocletian amused himself by working in his garden, and when Maximian sought to draw him from his retirement he wrote: "If you could see the cabbages I have planted with my own hand, you would never ask me to remount the throne." 305 A.D.

The soil intended for this general favorite should be deeply dug and *well dressed* with manure, and to prevent "club root" do not plant cabbage two successive seasons on the same soil and do not use hog manure. A dressing of lime will sometimes pay. In manuring soil for cabbage put the manure on until you are sure there is enough and then put on two or three times as much more, and then you will probably have enough.

Two distinct crops are, or should be, grown in every garden. They are "early" and "late." Seed of the earliest sorts is sown from February to March and April, which will be ready for use about four months from time of sowing. Therefore we may now enjoy this vegetable almost as early as we formerly could from seed sown the September previous, and do not have the plants to care for during the winter.

In setting out the plants care should be exercised to set them down to the first leaves and thereby prevent the frost from splitting the stems and injuring them as it would otherwise do. Successional sowings may be made if circumstances require. Sow seed in hot bed or cold frame at dates given above, transplanting the seedlings to about two inches apart, or they will become tall and spindling—drawn. Give plenty of light and air. The old way of raising late cabbage was to burn a brush heap and while the ashes were warm the seed was sown therein. This is an old and good way where practicable. In transplanting to the open choose a showery day, but if it is hot and dry, water generously by pouring water on the roots and cover this wet soil with some that is fine and dry. This will prevent the soil from crusting around the plants and thus injure them. Evening is a splendid time to do this work as the plants then receive the benefit of the water all night. Cover the roots with fine soil, packing it to them, or the plants may wash loose and rot off, and besides they will stand the drought much better when treated in this way. The distance varies with the variety, soil, etc. The small early varieties do well in rows 18 inches apart, and 15 inches between plants, while the late sorts should be at least two feet asunder each way.

Cabbage must have good care to be a success, and must not be left to the care of the fairies and to the ravages of the worms, as often seems to be the case. About the third week in November the heads should be pulled on a dry day and left to drain, with the heads down; they should now be set on a dry spot, heads down as before, in rows by setting three heads together side by side, while if you wish, two more rows may be set on top of these.

Be careful to wrap the outside leaves around the heads to keep them clean and protect the heads. Soil is then thrown on them to the depth of five or six inches, packing it down firmly to prevent the rain and melting snow from soaking in. On the approach of winter cover the mound with salt hay or corn stalks, to keep out the frost. Rats like to work in vegetable mounds, where they will do considerable damage if not destroyed.

Red Cabbages are used principally for pickling purposes. Cabbage as well as other vegetables retain their flavor much better when stored as above, than when packed in the cellar to rot and pollute the air. Or it may be preserved to a certainty by tying a string around the stalk and suspending them from the top of the cellar. In this case the cellar must be cool and dry. Or the heads may be cut off and packed in a barrel, taking care to fill all spaces with chaff and keep in a dry cellar, or bury the barrel up to the top. Cover the top with a lid and straw to exclude frost when buried outside.

It must be understood that if the early sorts are wanted for winter use they must be sown later, as the cabbage, like every other vegetable, ripens in a certain number of days (this depends on the variety used) and is known by the falling off of the loose leaves, and when ripe soon begins to decay. The earliest matures in June. For second early the early varieties should be sown first of April and transplanted to the open ground in May. This crop should come to maturity in July or August.

The late varieties are sown in May and set out in July for winter use, or sown in February for early. When sown in May the crop matures in September, October and November, according to the variety used. If the plants are infested with lice, each handful should be dipped into tobacco dust or insect powder. Where it is desirable to economize space, lettuce or radish seed may be sown between the rows of early varieties, as it will be out of the way before the cabbage needs the ground. Excepting where they are wanted for summer use for pickling, or in cooler sections, the Red varieties will be more likely to succeed if sown in June for heading during the cool fall months.

SAVOY CABBAGE (*Brassica oleracea bullata*). Savoy Cabbages, as you are doubtless aware, have a superior flavor, especially when touched by frost. The culture required by

Savoys is much the same as that required in raising cabbage for a late crop.

You should make acquaintance with this real luxury of the cabbage family, for it is one of the most desirable of winter vegetables, as it answers two purposes; first, as a cabbage to be boiled, which is much sweeter than the common variety; second, as a beautiful, sweet salad cabbage when cut and dressed as is Endive.

This type of the *Brassica* family is not cultivated so generally with us as it is in Europe where its rare good quality is more fully appreciated. Unlike the common variety the leaves are much crumpled or blistered, owing to the fact that the tissue between the veins is much larger than is really necessary to fill the space and is bulged out and heavily wrinkled in accommodating itself to the limited space in which it has to grow. This tissue is the most delicious part of the plant and as the larger portion of the head is composed of this it makes the whole head of the most delicate flavor and of a marrowy nature when cooked.

They make the finest varieties for summer and fall, being especially desirable for boiling and for slaw. They also withstand the attacks of the worms better than the common varieties.

Carrot (*Daucus hortensis*).—This vegetable seems to have come to us from a time that is immemorial, and is another vegetable which is too little grown, as it is one of the best of products of the garden when prepared in various ways.

The carrot does best in a sandy loam which has been deeply dug and richly tilled. For an early crop sow as soon as the soil is in a proper condition. The seed should be sown in rows 12 inches apart, thinning so that the plants remaining are 4 to 6 inches apart. For late use sow at any time up to the middle of June. Carrot seed is one of those which is slow to germinate, and all precautions should be taken to prevent failure. The seed should be in all cases sown in rows, not more than one inch in depth, and the soil (which must be fine and mellow) well firmed about the seed; and to render the operation of sowing more easy it will be found of great advantage to mix the seed with sand.

Cultivate thoroughly and keep the soil clean and mellow. Allow the crop to remain in the soil as long as possible without danger of freezing to allow the roots to more thoroughly mature, as they will keep much better than when pulled before ripe. When pulled allow them to dry off before storing. Dig when the soil is dry, and store in sand or earth in the cellar or bury in the same manner as recommended for beets or other root crops, as they remain more fresh, crisp and tender when stored in this manner. A very slight frost injures Carrots more than other roots. Carrots also make a very nutritious and desirable food for stock, especially for milch cows, as the milk is richer and the butter is sweeter and of a more beautiful color.

While a sandy loam made rich by manuring a previous crop is best suited to the carrot, any good soil thoroughly and deeply tilled will produce good crops. Where the soil is shallow we would recommend the sowing of stump-rooted varieties. Where the Carrot is grown on a large scale, as in field culture, it will be found that a clover sod heavily dressed with thoroughly decayed manure will produce splendid crops.

Cauliflower (*Brassica oleracea botrytis cauliflora*).—This delicious vegetable must be well and carefully grown. Any soil that will grow *good* cabbage will grow this, the most delicious of all vegetables, though the richer the soil the better. Extra care will be well repaid.

Sow the seed in hot bed in February or March, transplanting the plants two or three inches apart in boxes, or in the soil of another hot bed, giving an abundance of light and air on fine days until such a time as it is safe to plant in the open soil, which is from the last of March to the middle of April, according to the location of your vicinity; further south earlier, further north later.

The plants will stand a light frost if hardened off properly before setting them in the open ground. If properly hardened they are seldom injured by planting out too early. For second early and late crop sow at the dates given for cabbage. The soil intended for this crop should be very rich, turned over in the autumn, and a heavy dressing of manure applied and worked in, and the whole left to the action of the frost. It should be thoroughly broken up in the spring and got into a friable condition.

It will greatly improve the appearance of the heads if the broad outside leaves are bent over them while the curds are forming, keeping them white and attractive. The heads should be cut while the dew is on them and before the buds uncurl, as this improves this, the most deliciously flavored member of the cabbage family.

Never buy cheap Cauliflower seed. It's a snare.

It must be borne in mind, however, that Cauliflower will not head in hot, dry weather, hence the sowings must be made so that they will mature in cool, moist weather. Give *thorough* culture and *keep free from worms*.

The secret to Cauliflower culture is to get them started right. They will not always grow where cabbage will succeed, at least that is the author's experience. Do not allow the plants to crowd each other in the seed bed. Transplanting frequently, giving more room each time is essential.

Cauliflower requires a moist soil in connection with a cool moist atmosphere. The best Cauliflower seed comes from Denmark. Mulch the late ones. Work a little salt into the soil around the plants when cultivating them. This attracts moisture.

Cauliflower may be kept in the cellar until February by covering the roots and stalks with soil; or they may be placed in a trench roots down, and the trench filled with soil up to the heads, and the heads covered with hay or straw deep enough to keep out the frost.

Celery (*Apium Graveolens*).—This delicious, healthful and appetizing vegetable has come so generally into use that there is scarcely a garden that does not have a patch devoted to its growth. Where the soil is rich (and it must be to insure success) and the plants are well cared for, your Celery will be one of the most highly prized products of your garden.

The seed is slow to germinate and should be sown in shallow boxes, or in a thoroughly prepared, very rich bed, in a sunny nook in the garden as early as possible in April, or for winter use about a month later. Leave half of this bed vacant for use when the plants are large enough for their first transplanting, or when they are about two inches high. Keep the bed moist—almost wet—until the seed germinates, as plenty of moisture is necessary to obtain a satisfactory growth. Apply the water carefully so as not to wash the bed; dashing it on will not do.

Sow the seed (which is very small) in drills six inches apart, covering it but slightly, if at all; press it down firmly. Cultivate and keep free from weeds, and when about two inches high transplant them two or three inches apart.

This crop usually succeeds some other crop, such as early beans, peas, potatoes, etc., but in this case the soil must be very rich; the key to success in the culture of Celery is *very* rich soil and plenty of moisture. If large stocky plants are used they may be set out the early part of August, but I prefer to do this the last of June or the first of July. Much depends on your local climate, and should be so arranged that the plants will mature in cool, moist weather.

The plants must not be disturbed while wet, as this will greatly injure them. The new system of Celery culture consists of making a spot as rich as possible, and there setting the plants from six to eight inches apart each way. The plants are then blanched without further care, but the quality is inferior to that grown as of old.

In the old mode of culture when the plants are five or six inches high cut off the tops (which will cause them to grow stocky) and transplant into trenches twelve inches deep and about a foot wide at the top and eight inches at the bottom, having the soil banked up on each side. The bottom of the trench should be covered six inches deep with very fine manure or compost upon which is two or three inches of fine soil on which the plants are set. In dry weather a good soaking of water or the washing suds is essential; the latter is the best material that can be used. Shade the plants a few days until well rooted. This may be done by driving stakes along the rows and broad boards laid on these. About the 15th of August it is advisable to commence "earthing up," necessary for the proper blanching; then, too, Celery grows faster after the stalks are straightened up and the soil drawn around them, and packed firmly enough to keep them in an upright position. For this reason it is best to commence banking it early to give it an upright growth.

Be careful not to cover the hearts with soil nor to allow it to get among the stalks, for they will not thrive in the former case while in the latter they will be difficult to clean for use. In banking keep the ridge flat on top, to aid in blanching later on, and cultivate the soil thoroughly between the rows. The banking process must be repeated as the plants grow. Always select a dry day and when the soil is just damp enough to pack, taking care that no soil gets among the leaves.

It also aids in blanching to have the plants a little below the level, as in trenches. The self-blanching varieties are not as good keepers as the others; some of them not keeping longer than Christmas. When the last "earthing up" has been made, the soil must be beaten tolerably firm to throw off the rains.

When severe frosts set in a covering of some kind must be placed over the tops of the ridges to protect the plants. This must be done gradually as the cold increases. A trough may be inverted on the top of the ridge to hold the covering in place. Another and easier way to blanch it is to set the plants on the level ground, although the first way is the best in hot, dry seasons if the trenches are made running east and west, thereby shading the plants from the rays of the sun, which is very beneficial. But if the plants are set on the level, which does away with much hard labor, the easiest way to blanch the crop is by "boarding up," which is simply setting a board of the proper height on each side of the row close up to the plants, on its edge and held in position by stakes. When properly blanched your crop may be dug and is ready to market or store away for winter.

The following method is one which we can recommend where the weather is too severe to allow the crop to remain where grown: Set the plants as closely together as the bunches of the roots will allow without crowding, upon and partially in a layer of moist soil, in the corner of the cellar. Keep the roots moist and the tops dry, using the plants that are most nearly blanched first. Instead of setting directly on the cellar floor, you may place them in boxes of convenient size, having soil in the bottom. Bore a few holes in the sides of the box, through which you can apply water as needed.

Celeriac is grown similar to celery when that crop is grown on the surface and is used as a salad or in seasoning. Transplant the plants to moist, rich soil in rows two feet apart and six inches in the rows. Give good cultivation. It is more hardy than celery and as the roots are the edible part of this vegetable banking is not necessary, but recommended. When the bulbs are two inches in diameter they are ready for use. The roots are preserved for winter similar to beets, carrots, etc. It makes a delicious salad when cooked and sliced with vinegar.

Celery rust is occasioned by anything that injures the roots—a long drought or an excess of water which kills the working roots, and the yellowing up or rusting of the leaves soon follows. This delicious delicacy is said to have originated in Germany.

Chives. These are entirely hardy perennials, and are of the onion family, grown exclusively for their tops which are used wherever the flavor of the onion is required. It also makes a fine effect when planted among bedding plants. Plant in small clumps in good soil and keep free from weeds.

They grow quickly and in time the clump will need to be divided. Being entirely hardy they appear quite early and may be cut throughout the season. The tops only are used and if not allowed to flower will produce much longer.

Chicory (*Cichorium intybus*).—This is closely related to our winter Endive (*Cichorium endivia*) and grows from two to three feet high, has sky-blue flowers and in some sections is found in fields and by the wayside. It makes an excellent winter salad when blanched. The seeds are sown in May in drills three-fourths of an inch deep and fifteen inches apart.

It requires a rich, mellow soil of good depth. When two or three inches high the plants should be thinned to eight inches apart. The soil requires frequent cultivation and should be kept absolutely clear of weeds. To blanch them, boxes or flower pots about twelve inches deep should be turned over the plants. When wanted for winter use the plants are taken up late in the fall, and planted closely in boxes of light soil or sand and then placed in a cool cellar, watering them after planting. When wanted for use a box of them should be placed in a warm room, where the temperature will be from 50° to 60°. Growth will soon commence.

Many people like the flavor of coffee better where a little chicory or succory has been added. Where it is grown for this purpose the plants should be fully grown. The roots are then cut into small pieces, and roasted to a good coffee color, and then it may be mixed with the coffee or used separately in making that world-renowned beverage.

Collards.—These originated in the south where they are extensively grown, as they are a sure, easy crop and afford an abundance of food for both man and beast. Collards are the result of the effort of the cabbage to perpetuate itself under an adverse climate. It forms a quantity of leaves on a tall stem, which are much improved by being touched by frost. It grows quickly and is a staple form of "greens" in the south but not much cultivated in the north. The new "Blue Stem" variety produces fine blanched heads which are of more delicate flavor than the old variety. As the leaves are gathered the plant continues to grow and produce new leaves in abundance. In the southern states growth continues throughout the winter, but in the northern states the weather is too severe.

The Collard is cultivated winter and summer in rows not less than three feet apart; is a very exhaustive feeder and must have very rich soil and should not be grown on the same soil two successive seasons. The heading may be greatly facilitated by bending the plants over and covering the stems and some of the lower leaves with soil, which tends to check the rampant growth and cause the leaves in the center to form finer heads. This should be done after the first light frosts.

Corn Salad.—This is a hardy plant, and is one of the most economical of all small salads, and may be used as a substitute for lettuce in winter. It may also be cooked and served as is spinach.

For early spring use the seed is sown in August, and in April for summer use. Sow in rows one foot apart, covering the seeds lightly. As this plant reaches maturity in about four weeks in summer, a succession of sowings will be necessary where this plant is relished. Cultivate same as spinach, and protect from frost by a light covering of leaves or litter which may be held in place by a few branches. Of no value in the hot summer months.

Sugar Corn.—Every garden large or small should contain a full supply of this universal favorite for table use, for who is there that does not enjoy a plentiful supply of "roastin' ears."

The early varieties should be planted as soon as possible after the soil has become warm and the weather settled; or about the time field corn is planted; or earlier, taking chances. To have the finest sweet corn of any variety it should be picked in just the right condition; that is, when the skin breaks at the slightest puncture, and plantings should be so made as to always have a supply at this stage. The quality is inferior if a few days too old or too young. It will be well to remember that the early kinds are as a rule of poor quality, as they lack the richness of the later kinds, yet there are exceptions to even this rule as in everything else.

Prepare the soil thoroughly in everyway and use plenty of seed, as the early sorts do not exceed three feet in height. A little compost mixed with the soil will help it along. The best is raised on a shale. When the ears are gathered cut the fodder or it will soon go to waste. The whole maize family requires warm, rich soil to do its best, and will not make any headway until the weather is settled and will be very likely to rot; sweet corn especially will decay where common field corn will grow and the purer and sweeter the seed the less hardships it will bear. Always select a warm soil if possible, especially for the earlier varieties, as the difference in soil and exposure will make at least a week's difference in the time of maturity, besides insuring a crop.

All varieties of sweet corn may be sown in rows four feet apart and the grains placed eight or ten inches apart in the rows. This is best for early sorts for when planted at the regular distances, three or four feet each way, too much room is wasted, but the distance should be regulated according to the variety planted or the richness of the soil. The taller the variety or the richer the soil the greater should be the distance apart. Continue planting every two or three weeks until the last of July when a crop may be secured by planting an early sort.

Always select the long deep grains for seed purposes whenever possible; by doing this you will always raise a better crop of finer quality than otherwise. Select those varieties having a white cob, as the silks are also white making it easier to prepare and giving it a finer appearance when cooked or dried than those having dark cobs and silks.

An excellent way to boil corn is to boil it with a portion of the husks remaining on the ears. Remove the silks and tough outer husks, leaving the white inner leaves only. The corn will be much sweeter if cooked in this way. Parched sweet corn is quite palatable.

It must be borne in mind that sugar corn must be planted at some distance from field corn and pop corn or they will cross and the quality of your sugar corn will be greatly deteriorated. The exact distance at which they should be from each other cannot be given here as circumstances differ, but it must be considerable as the pollen is very light and is carried by the wind, bees, etc., long distances.

Pop Corn.—This should be grown in every garden, especially if there are little ones in the family to enjoy it during the long winter evenings, which bring children together for social enjoyment while older people as well seem to have no objections to "poppin' " some corn. It is a fact not generally known that it does not arrive at its best for popping until it is a year or more old, and, that when well popped it becomes nearly twenty times its natural size.

The white rice is generally considered the best variety but a variety of kinds is attractive. Cultivate similar to field corn. The soil should be rich and mellow. Plant in rows three feet apart and fifteen inches between the hills, three stalks to a hill; 50 to 100 bushels of forty pound each may be grown on one acre.

Great care must be exercised in keeping pop corn entirely isolated from either field corn or sugar corn while growing, as mixing with these will spoil its popping qualities. Be careful to store it away from mice.

A great amount of pleasure may be derived from popping and preparing it in various ways on the long winter evenings that drag so on the "folks at home," and, too, it keeps the young folks at home when otherwise they might seek entertainment at the village.

An Excellent way to Pop Corn.—Into a vessel of lard, heated as for frying cakes, put half a pint of shelled pop corn, and cover the vessel to prevent the corn from popping out. Care must be taken that the corn does not burn. When done, take it out with a skimmer and drain thoroughly on a sieve over a pan. Salt to suit the taste.

To make Pop Corn Balls.—The corn must be well popped; all that is not nicely popped should be discarded. Place one-half bushel of the corn in a large dripping pan. Into a suitable kettle put one pound of sugar with a little water and boil as for candy until it becomes quite waxy in water; then remove from the fire and dip into it seven tablespoons of thick gum solution, made by pouring boiling water upon gum arabic some hours before needed. Now dip the mixture upon different parts of the corn. With the hands or a stick mix the corn until thoroughly saturated with the syrup or candy mixture; then make into balls, being quick or it will set before you get through. The above will make about one hundred balls. White or brown sugar may be used. For variety white sugar may be used for a portion and molasses for another part. When making balls pop the corn in the usual manner, without the lard.

Cress (*Lenidium sativum*).—A justly popular and very appetizing salad plant which should be sown in early spring, very thickly in shallow drills, and at frequent intervals for succession, as it soon runs to seed. It will bear cutting several times during the season. Used mixed with lettuce its leaves impart an agreeable, warm, pungent taste. The leaves should be cut while young and tender to be palatable.

WATER CRESS is a hardy, perennial, aquatic plant which thrives best along the banks of running streams or ponds or in other moist situations, the former being best suited to its growth. The plants increase rapidly from extensions of the roots and from self-sown seed from year to year. This is one of the most appetizing, delicious flavored of all small salads and grows luxuriantly on the edges of shallow streams as above stated. The seed may be sown in May where the plants are to remain, and the thinnings transplanted and should be set not less than a foot apart. The Cress will be ready for gathering the second season. The leaves are quite large and thick.

UPLAND CRESS is a perennial resembling Water Cress in flavor, is good all the year round and is recommended for dry localities where Water Cress will not thrive. Cut often while the leaves are young and tender, as they then possess a pleasant, pungent flavor that is quite agreeable.

Cucumber (*Cucumis Satavus*).—This is one of the vegetables mentioned in early bible history for we read of it in Numbers xi, 5, and Isaiah i, 8, while it grows abundantly in Egypt, and is common in Palestine, being grown by acres on the plains, and is the staple article of vegetable diet of the poor, during summer. They are also a great relish with us, as an appetizer, and are quite tender as are all semi-tropical plants.

Cucumbers require a rich, sandy soil, the hills being made about three feet apart. These are best made by mixing rich, very fine manure in the soil where the hill is to be.

A splendid way to raise an early supply without expense and with little labor, is to dig out a hole large enough to hold a wheelbarrowful of manure, finely pulverized; cover this with five inches of fine, rich soil, and plant the seeds in this, covering about one inch deep. Keep the soil moist to keep it from crusting and to germinate the seeds. These hills should, however, be in a warm sunny nook to insure success.

For an ordinary crop prepare the soil as directed at the beginning of this subject. Sow in May for early use and the 15th of June for pickles. The vines will bear more abundantly if the tips of the leading shoots are pinched off when the vines are about one foot in length. When all danger from bugs is over thin out the plants, leaving not more than three or four to each hill. The fruit should be gathered when large enough whether required for use or not, for if permitted to ripen on the vines it will destroy their productiveness, for the vines having filled their natural tendencies—that of preserving the species—soon wither and die. Keep the soil mellow and free from weeds and draw a little around the stems from time to time as the vines advance in growth.

White Spine is a favorite with some in many respects, especially for market, as they retain a greenish tinge even when nearly ripe for seed. These like all others are best when picked while young and brittle.

The spaces between the hills of Cucumbers, as well as melon and squash hills, may be occupied by pepper plants as they grow above the foliage of the vines and require very little room, and will receive the benefit of the moisture which is retained in the soil by the shade afforded by the vines. This also economizes space. White varieties are quite attractive.

Forcing Cucumbers.—This method is sometimes resorted to where a few *extra early* Cucumbers are desired. It may be somewhat tedious to the average gardener, and while the directions given above are ample for ordinary use, we will give a few directions for those who wish to try them. First, procure a variety suited to frame culture. Any kind will do, but some are more suited to this purpose than are others.

Now prepare your hot bed in February or March. In two or three days after preparing the bed the soil will be sufficiently warm for sowing the seed; now place a wheelbarrowful of rich, fine soil in the center of the sash, in the form of a mound; on this sow several seeds to allow for those that may damp off as sometimes happens in cloudy weather. If all grow, thin to four plants. Place the pointed end of the seed down, covering about one inch deep. Cover the sash with straw, old carpets, or litter, or other protection to prevent the heat from escaping, and, too, the bed should be surrounded with manure for same reason. The seed will sprout in a day or two, and in a week or ten days will form strong plants. During growth give plenty of air whenever the weather permits, being careful that the temperature does not fall below 60°.

Keep them growing vigorously without too much forcing. When they have formed three rough leaves nip off the tip of the plant. This will cause them to branch. If the soil becomes dry water with luke-warm water. As growth progresses, roots will start from the vines and through the hill, to which rich soil should be placed. The surface roots will soon find their way through this and the whole surface of the bed will soon be covered with foliage, flowers and fruit. Syringing every day will prove quite beneficial. A soaking of weak, liquid manure at least once a week will aid in making a vigorous growth.

Or, the seeds may be sown in pots half filled with light, rich soil, and plunged to the rim in the hot bed or greenhouse. Fill up the pots as the plants grow, and when they have attained some growth they should be shifted into larger pots and finally placed in the frames in which plants have been wintered, as these will be empty in May or June. Place the frame where good drainage is insured, and place a barrowful of rich soil in the frame as directed above.

In planting be careful not to injure the roots, and keep the bed closed and shaded until well established. As soon as fruit appears the shoot bearing it should have the tip pinched out and every fruit cut as soon as large enough, for if any are allowed to ripen, the vine, having filled its natural design, will soon wither and die. Large specimens look well when on exhibit, but are exhausting to the plant. In the heat of the day a light sprinkle of straw or leaves over the sash will prevent the plants from drooping.

The GHERKIN is raised similar to outdoor cucumbers. The fruits are small, oval and covered with spines; color light green, while the vine closely resembles that of the watermelon. Excellent for pickles when gathered while quite small.

When gathering vine fruits exercise care in so doing if you want the vines to continue bearing. Nip off the fruit leaving the stem attached. A slight pull will loosen the vine from the soil thus injuring it.

Protect your crop from insect pests by dusting the plants with dust or soot while wet with dew; and plant a few radish, turnip or cabbage seeds in each hill to guard them against the small black flea.

Fruits should be cut early in the morning or in the evening, using a sharp knife or shears, taking care not to injure the vines.

Dandelion (*Taraxacum officinale*).—The Dandelion resembles endive and affords one of the earliest as well as one of the most wholesome spring greens. Sow the seed in May or June in fine mellow soil in rows one foot apart, cover the seed one-half inch deep and firm the soil well over them. Thin the plants so that they will stand one foot apart each way. Cultivate during the summer, which will make the roots larger and considerable time will be saved when trimming or gathering the crop which will be ready for use the following spring. The Dandelion has rather a bitter taste and should have the first water poured from them while cooking. They are quite healthful.

Endive (*Cichorium Endivia*).—This salad, though seldom grown, is one of the most valuable salad plants we have for fall and winter use. The first sowing of Endive should be made in April and successive sowings may be made once a month up to the end of August. The first sowing will best succeed on a warm border and should be transplanted one foot apart each way; or if preferred they may be thinned to the desired distance.

Later sowings may be made in any part of the garden providing the soil is rich and light. If this is the case the Batavian varieties must be 15 inches apart each way. When the plants are grown tie the outside leaves over the heart to blanch the inner leaves—5 to 10 days are required for this. This must not be done, however, when the plants are damp or they will soon decay. When properly grown this is one of the most appetizing of all salads, while if boiled like spinach it is relished by some.

Egg Plant (*Solanum esculentum*).—This grand, good delicacy is too little grown, as it is one of the most delicious vegetables we have, and should be in every garden as it will thrive with good care in any good soil, and will repay good cultivation.

The seeds are sown in hot beds and require considerable heat to germinate them, for as this is a sub-tropical plant it is of importance that they make a rapid growth from the first, as they never recover from a check received while young. Repeated sowings are sometimes necessary.

Keep very warm and partially shaded, giving plenty of water until the weather is settled and the ground warm, and all danger from cold nights is past; then harden the plants by gradual exposure to the sun and air and diminish the amount of water. Sow in March and when they have attained the second rough leaf transplant two or three inches apart, handling carefully. It is a very tender plant and care must be used when they are set out or they will be chilled by the change. This and tomato plants are second choice of the potato bug which will destroy them if not checked. Set in rows two feet apart each way in *very* rich soil, and give every advantage possible. If needed shade the plants until well established, and draw the soil up to their stems as they advance in growth.

Pick the eggs as soon as large enough as the quality deteriorates as they begin to ripen. When well grown your Egg Plants will be one of the most highly prized products of the garden. They should have the richest soil possible from the seed bed throughout their entire growth. When gathering the "eggs" care should be observed so as not to disturb the roots of the plants or they will be severely damaged. In the more northerly states this vegetable must have every care to succeed. Gather the fruits before the seeds harden. On the approach of frost gather all fruits that are large enough for use as they will keep for a considerable length of time.

In the summer when the soil is liable to become dry it may be kept moist by placing a mulch of hay or straw around the roots of the plants to a depth of two or three inches.

Garlic (*Allium Sativum*).—This is the most pungent of the onion tribe and not much used except by the Germans and for medicine. The history of this vegetable dates back into antiquity, as we find it mentioned in Numbers XI, 5, and was one of the vegetables enjoyed by the Israelites in Egyptian bondage; while Herodotus (450 B. C.) writes that in his time there was an inscription on the great pyramid telling of the 16,000 talents that were spent for onion, leek and garlic, with which to feed the builders of the pyramid.

The roots are composed of several divisions called "cloves." These are separated in the spring and planted as are onion sets, in rows two feet apart and six inches in the rows. Do not allow the plants to run to seed stalk. This may be prevented by breaking down the tops or by tying them in a knot. In the autumn when ripe, pull and tie together in bunches and put away for future use.

Horse Radish.—This favorite vegetable may be grown in any garden soil, but a moist situation is best suited to its growth. The best shaped roots are grown from the small roots, and not from the tops or crowns. These sets planted in spring in rich, moist soil will produce roots of large size the first season.

Before setting, the tops are cut off slantingly to prevent water from standing on them and causing them to decay. Some advise digging in the fall before the ground freezes and storing in trenches, or in sand in the cellar. This may do in some cases but I would prefer to dig as needed, as they retain their strength and aroma better.

From the large roots a supply of sets may be secured for planting. Horse Radish is a difficult plant to eradicate when once established, and therefore had best be kept under control.

In planting the sets a trowel may be used, or they may be planted by driving the spade full length into the soil flat to the garden line and moved back and forth to make a hole; two sets may be placed in this, one at each side. Press the soil to them and you are sure of success as this vegetable is sure to grow almost regardless of conditions. This is a favorite relish and one that is quite wholesome and appetizing.

Herbs.—A small plot of Sweet Herbs and Pot Herbs should be found in every vegetable garden, be it large or small, for every good housewife knows the value of a small patch of herbs upon which she can make daily visits in the summer and which furnishes such a nice collection of seasoning for winter use, and without which the Thanksgiving and Christmas turkey would be scarcely worth the having; while as domestic medicines many are held in high repute. A very small patch is sufficient for the requirements of the average family.

Their culture is very simple, as follows: Sow the seed in a seed bed of rich earth in a corner of the garden in early spring and transplant into rows as soon as they have attained sufficient size. On the average the rows should be at least 18 inches apart and about a foot between the plants. Herbs in general thrive best in a mellow and free soil and care should be exercised in properly harvesting them in a dry state. The chief points are to cut them on a dry day just before they come into full bloom and to dry them quickly in the shade; when thoroughly dry pack them closely in dry, air-tight boxes, keeping them entirely excluded from the air.

Some of them are perennial and when once obtained in the garden may be preserved for many years with a little care in summer and slight protection during winter. They should be in a bed to themselves where they will not interfere with the management of the rest of the garden.

Many people still grow the simple medicinal herbs for home use. Seed of those of which the leaves are used either in green or dry state, perennial varieties especially, should be sown thinly in shallow drills as early as the soil can be made fine and mellow, as the seeds germinate better in cool, moist weather. The perennials should be transplanted to permanent beds on the borders where they will not interfere with cultivation of the remainder of the garden. The annuals should also be sown early, making the rows 18 inches apart and setting the plants about one foot apart in the rows for such varieties as are grown for their leaves, and two feet apart for those producing aromatic seeds. The former should be cut and dried as given above, while the seed heads of the latter should be cut as soon as ripened and spread in a cool airy room or tied in small bundles, and may be threshed and cleaned, when they are ready for use.

Below we give a list of the most common varieties with the manner of using. The following are annuals:

ANISE (*Pimpinella anisum*)—Used for cordial, flavoring; the seeds are aromatic. BALM (*Melissa officinalis*)—Leaves have a fragrant odor; used in making balm wine, also for balm tea for use in fevers. BASIL (*Ocymum basilicum*)—Leaves are used for flavoring soups and other highly seasoned dishes. BENE (*Sesamum orientale*)—The leaves immersed in water make a drink very beneficial in cases of diarrhoea, while the seeds furnish an oil used for softening the skin. BORAGE (*Borago officinalis*)—Leaves are used for flavoring; flowers for bee pasture. CORIANDER (*Coriandrum savitum*)—The seeds only are used. DILL (*Anethum graveolens*)—The seeds are aromatic and of a warm, pungent taste. Used as seasoning; also for pickling. MARJORAM (*Origanum marjoram*)—The leaves and ends of shoots are used for seasoning both green and dry. SAVORY, summer (*Satureia hortensis*)—Leaves and blossoms are used for flavoring, especially soups and dressings.

The following varieties are of perennial nature and remain in the ground for years with slight protection in winter:

CARAWAY (*Carum carui*)—Seeds used for flavoring bread, pastry, etc. FENNEL, sweet (*Anethum foeniculum*)—The boiled leaves are used in fish sauces. HOREHOUND (*Marrubium vulgare*)—Leaves used for seasoning and in the manufacture of the favorite cough remedy. LAVENDER (*Lavendula vera*)—Aromatic, medicinal. PENNYROYAL (*Mentha pulegium*)—But little known. Of a bright green suited for growing on rockwork. ROSEMARY (*Rosmarinus officinalis*)—Leaves aromatic; used for seasoning. SAGE (*Salvia officinalis*)—See Sage culture. SAVORY, winter (*Satureia montana*)—Leaves and tender shoots used for flavoring. TANSY (*Tanacetum vulgare*)—For medicinal purposes. *Tagetes Lucida.*—Very pretty, and an excellent substitute for tarragon. THYME (*Thymus vulgaris*)—Leaves and tender shoots used for flavoring; a tea is also made for nervous headache. WORMWOOD (*Artemisia absinthium*)—Medicinal; good for poultry. TARRAGON (*Artemisia dracunculus*)—Used for seasoning or salads. The stems may be cut and dried. Must have protection in the north. Increased by layering or from slips. SAFFRON (*Crocus sativus*)—Flowers used for dyeing; also used medicinally. CATNIP or CATMINT (*Nepeta cataria*)—Leaves and young shoots used for seasoning and for "Catnip tea." RUE (*Ruta graveolens*)—Medicinal. Good for fowls, for colds and croup.

Kohl Rabi (*Brassica oleracea caulo-rapa*).—This like okra and many other vegetables is too little appreciated by many, for when properly prepared it is one of the most desirable, as it combines the virtues of both the cabbage and turnip, but excels either in productiveness, hardiness and quality. Seed should be sown in drills 15 inches apart and transplant the surplus ones into rows 8 inches between the plants.

Choose a rainy day for this, as they are considered difficult to transplant.

Sow at intervals of 10 days for a succession until hot weather, when they fail to grow well. Those sown for winter use should be sown in July, and for the reasons given will do better if thinned to the proper distance. The bulb should be used while young—about the size of an orange—as age detracts from its good quality. They may be preserved for winter use as are beets and carrots, and are improved by being frozen before they are gathered.

Leek (*Allium Porrum*).—Aside from being valuable for soups and salads, blanched Leek makes an excellent dish when sliced and cooked as are peas. This fact does not seem to be generally known, as Leeks are seldom seen in the average farmer's garden. They may be had all winter if dug with the roots on and stored in moist sand in the cellar.

Sow the seed very early, about March 1st, in a rich seed bed in a sheltered place. Keep well watered while in the seed bed. When six inches high transplant into trenches six inches deep, with very rich soil in the bottom. Fill up the trenches as the plants grow, and afterwards draw soil up to them. As a result you will have fine large Leeks 12 inches long that will tempt the palate of the epicure.

Perhaps few are aware that the Leek is one of the finest winter vegetables, and when properly grown can be had with from six inches to one foot of white which when boiled is very nutritious, and much milder than the onion. With a good supply of crisp and tender vegetables all carefully put into a root cellar, we are prepared to give a change of diet all winter as well as summer.

Lettuce (*Lactuca sativa*).—This valuable salad amply repays any trouble that may be bestowed on its cultivation. Lettuce is divided into two classes; the cabbage with round heads and the cos with long head and erect narrow leaves. The cabbage varieties are firmer, the most tender and buttery, while the latter are most refreshing.

Prepare the soil by digging deeply and manuring heavily, while after planting never allow the plants to suffer for water. Sow in the open ground as early as possible in drills one foot apart and as soon as large enough thin out or transplant to four inches apart; or if you have any plants from fall sowing, transplant into a rich bed and hoe well. If sown in hot bed let it be sown early, give but little heat and plenty of water. Sow a couple of rows quite thickly to be used while young.

For later use sow in a partially shaded place in rich soil and water freely. That which is sown early should be in a warm, sunny nook, continuing successive sowings every two or three weeks until July. Sow the hardy sorts in August or September for spring use, and protect with frames, leaves or litter, while if a few of the best plants are allowed to sow their own seed you will have an abundance of this delicious salad very early. Always keep the soil mellow and free from weeds, as this requires good care as much as any other crop.

There is no vegetable that is more universally used than is Lettuce and yet comparatively few persons know how inviting and appetizing it really is when brought to the table fresh, crisp and unwilted, a condition in which we scarcely ever find this really excellent salad in our markets, and which can only be secured by growing the plants in our own kitchen gardens. In fact this is the case with nearly all vegetables; the fresher they are the better will be their qualities. For this and various other reasons we urge all our friends to have at least a small vegetable patch and to raise a full supply of deliciously crisp and tender garden "sass."

Melon, Musk (*Cucumis Melo*).—This, everybody's favorite, especially early ones, delights in a light, rich, sandy soil, and contrary to the common opinion is of easy cultivation. As to its early history we find it mentioned in Numbers XI, 5, while Pliny records its use, and as he died A. D. 79 we judge it is as old as the cucumber. They flourish in Egypt from May to November and grow very large and are a staple crop, refreshing to both the thirsty as well as the hungry. This refers to the watermelon.

If your soil is infested by cut worms plow as early as possible in the spring. Rake or harrow the manure into the soil and make the hills from 3x3 to 4½x4½ feet apart. These should be made very rich by thoroughly incorporating very fine manure into the soil.

The manure described for Watermelons is also splendid for these. Place a shovelful in each hill and tramp firmly; make a hill over this and sow the seed, putting six to eight in each hill. Cover about one inch deep and firm the soil above the seed. As soon as in rough leaf loosen the soil around the plants. Do not bruise the vines or they will be injured. When the plants are 6 to 8 inches high, rake with a wooden rake and hoe again. Keep the soil mellow and destroy grass and weeds. The striped bug may cause trouble and damage to the young plants, and must be kept in check. (See the chapter on injurious insects.)

Muskmelons are very tender and will not bear rough usage. Neither should they be handled when wet. As soon as the plants are large enough to care for themselves thin down to three or four of the most promising. Pinch off the tips of the leading shoots if the growth becomes too vigorous. If the fruits set too thickly, thin out when young. This will increase the size of the remaining ones and cause them to ripen earlier. They have reached maturity when they will leave the vine under slight pressure. The quality is best when the fruits are ripened in the shade.

Gather as soon as ready or the hot sun will soon spoil them. Sickly vines, unsuitable soil or unfavorable weather will produce fruit of poor flavor. Keep the vines growing vigorously from the start.

Melon, Water (*Cucurbita citrullus*).—Watermelons thrive best in a warm, sandy loam. They grow best in a clover sod of the above texture. As cut worms abound it is best to plow in the autumn or early in the spring.

With good soil and plenty of manure to place in the hills success is reasonably assured. Place a shovelful in each hill and cover about four inches deep with fine soil. Make the hills about 6x6 feet. As to the manure best suited to their growth I think horse and hog manure half and half; or the scrapings from the barnyard make a most excellent fertilizer. This must be well incorporated with the soil or it will burn the plants and cause a failure. The seeds, six or eight in number to each hill, are covered with fine mellow soil one inch deep. This should be firmly packed over the seeds. Do not allow the soil to crust.

Cultivate thoroughly to keep the soil loose and free from weeds. Sow as early as possible using an early kind. Seed three or four years old is said to be better than strictly fresh seed as it gives more solid flesh with fewer seeds. Handle the vines carefully and do not tread on them when gathering the melons as this is certain to injure them.

"Do not plant too close to pumpkins or squashes or they will hybridize and spoil your melons" is what some people say, but I have never known this to happen although it may be a fact. The essential points for success are: Suitable soil, pure seed, good culture, plenty of manure, and good strong vines early in the season. When the Melons have arrived at maturity the quirl nearest the Melons will have died. By this you will know when they are ripe without plugging them. Care must be exercised that watermelons and citrons or preserving melons are not planted in close proximity or they will cross and spoil both crops.

Mustard (*Sinapis alba* (white) and *Sinapis nigra* (black).—This is a hardy plant and is used as a salad in early spring and is very appetizing, being slightly warm to the taste. In England mustard and cress mixed is used as a salad and is one of their table delicacies. In this case water cress is preferable.

Seed of this vegetable is sown as soon as the frost is out of the ground in shallow drills one foot apart and one-half inch deep in mellow soil. The plants will soon present themselves and be ready for use as they must be used while young and tender, for when old they become unfit for use. If mustard is desired for winter use allow the plants to run to seed. These should be gathered before the seed begins to scatter, dried, threshed and ground. When using this "home grown" mustard it should be mixed with vinegar and allowed to stand a while before using. If this is neglected the mustard will have a bitter taste, owing, I suppose, to the fact that the skin of the seed is not removed as is the case with that which we buy. The black mustard is used for this purpose.

Do not allow seed to scatter on your ground as it is quite hardy and will spread and become difficult to eradicate. *Sinapis N.* is supposed to be the plant referred to in Mathew XIII, 31; but this is not certain.

Mushrooms (*Agaricus campestris*) or Common Variety.—Of this fungi there are a great many species. Around the growth of this highly esteemed and nutritious esculent there seems to be a profound mystery which can be penetrated only by the initiated; in reality, however, it is a very simple matter, requiring only ordinary intelligence and care. They can be grown in any dark room or cellar where the temperature can be maintained at about 50° or 60°.

From some old pasture obtain the soil and store it away. To one bushel of this add two bushels of fresh horse manure. Of this mixture prepare a bed four feet wide and of the length desired. Put down a thin layer of this and pack it firmly, proceeding in this manner until you have a bed eight inches thick. This will soon become quite hot, but allow the heat to recede to 85° or 90°. Then make holes about one foot apart each way and place the spawn in these —two or three pieces the size of a small egg in each hole.

Cover this and press the soil solid and smooth. Let the bed remain in this condition for ten or twelve days; then cover the bed with two inches of loam. Over this place four or five inches of hay or straw and the work is complete.

If the work is properly done, in six or eight weeks you may reap your reward. The bed will continue in bearing twenty or thirty days. After gathering the crop spread an inch of fresh soil over the bed, moisten with warm water and cover as before. But success depends so much upon a proper and uniform moisture, temperature and other atmospherical conditions that success is not always certain with the beginner. In market there is always a demand and an over supply is seldom known.

Other edible varieties are: *Marasmius oreades* (Fairy Ring), *Coprinus comatus* (horse tail·), *Cantharellus cibarius*, *Chanterelle*, and many others.

To DISTINGUISH MUSHROOMS FROM POISONOUS FUNGI.—Sprinkle a little salt on the gills or under side of the umbrella. If they turn black they are edible; if yellow they are poisonous. *Allow the salt to act before you decide.* Poisonous mushrooms or fungi have a warty cap, or else fragments of membrane adhering to the upper surface, and emerge from a bag; they are also heavy while the mushroom proper is quite light. They also grow in tufts or clusters in the woods, on the stumps of trees, etc., while the true edible mushrooms grow in old pastures late in the summer. False mushrooms or toadstools have an astringent, styptic and disagreeable taste. They are moist on the surface and generally of a rose or orange color, and when cut they turn blue. The gills of the true mushroom are of a pinky red, changing to a liver color, while the flesh is white. The stem is white, solid and cylinderical with the ring a little more than half way up. The above rules hold good to those who are in the habit of gathering wild mushrooms.

Okra.—This is an annual from the West Indies and like many others is seldom seen in the garden; yet its young, green seed pods give a fine flavor and consistency to soups, etc., besides being very palatable when cooked and served as is asparagus. The pods while young and tender may also be dried for winter use. It is extensively grown throughout the southern states, and should be more generally cultivated in our northern gardens as it is as easily grown as a weed.

The plants, which bear large, white Hibiscus-like flowers with a deep maroon center, make a very pretty sight even in the flower garden. Okra is a vigorous plant requiring considerable space. The large variety should be planted three feet apart and the dwarf eighteen inches. In mild climates it is only necessary to sow the seed in the open garden about two inches deep and merely keep the soil clean and mellow as for a hill of corn, drawing the soil up to the stems as they advance in growth. The plants bear for a longer period if the pods are picked when of sufficient size. The surplus pods may also be dried for winter use by running a thread through them and hanging them up from the flies, in a cool place. They must be gathered while young or they will be woody. They can also be canned with tomatoes. A grand vegetable.

Onion (*Allium Cepa*).—This is another of the vegetables mentioned in Numbers xi, 5, as one of the vegetables of Egypt, where it is extensively grown near the Nile and in Syria, where it is eaten raw. The Egyptian variety is as large as the common Portugal variety.

The onion thrives best in a rather deep, rich, loamy soil, and unlike most crops succeeds best when grown on the same ground for several successive seasons. To grow onions successfully the soil cannot be made too rich and must have more or less manure well worked through the soil for every crop, for it is a plant producing numerous roots which reach out and penetrate deeply, absorbing sustenance from every part of the soil. This is a splendid crop to follow cabbage, yet as regards rotation the Onion occupies an anomalous place as the same soil has been known to produce splendid crops for many years. The soil should be plowed in the autumn, heavily manured and left as plowed so that the ridges will be exposed to the action of the frost. This crop must have a clean and very rich soil to succeed.

Use thoroughly decayed manure freely. This should be thoroughly incorporated with the soil before sowing the seed. Sow as early as possible in the spring no matter if the weather is cold and unpleasant, for if the Onion does not get a good start before the hot, dry weather the crop is sure to be a failure. Old seed will not produce a thrifty crop. Use new seed every time. Sow in drills one foot apart and one-half inch in depth, cover with fine soil and pressd own firmly. When the plants are large enough thin gradually so they will stand four inches apart, disturbing those remaining as little as possible. As Onions stand on top of the ground they may be allowed to grow pretty thickly, no matter if they do crowd each other. In hoeing just skim the surface of the soil keeping it level and do not cover the bulbs. Do not cultivate deeply but loosen the soil well up to the plants.

The Onion requires a firm seed bed or it is liable to make too many roots at the expense of the crop. Do not cover the bulbs with soil, for the more the Onion rises out of the soil the better it keeps when stored. When three inches high thin to two inches apart. Pull every other Onion for salading, leaving the remainder four inches apart. A top dressing of wood ashes after cultivating is very beneficial, as will be seen by the dark, healthy condition given to the plants, besides saving them from the ravages of the maggot. Where it is possible an application of dry, fine hen manure put on in the same way will be of great benefit to the crop. When the tops dry and fall the crop should be gathered at once for various reasons, and spread evenly on the ground to cure. When thoroughly dried the tops should be cut off half an inch from the bulb.

To grow pickling Onions the seed should be sown thickly on poor soil and allowed to grow without being thinned out.

As stated elsewhere in this article a good crop of Onions can be grown on any soil that will produce paying crops of other vegetables, unless it is a stiff clay, very light sand or gravel. Certain varieties of muck land will invariably produce stiff necks or "scallions" which are worthless on the market, as they do not form bulbs and do not ripen down well, while other muck soils produce large crops of the finest grade. The soil best suited to their growth is a rich, sandy loam with a light mixture of clay. It is also much better if it has been cultivated, kept clean and well manured for a year or two previous, for if a sufficient amount of manure to raise ordinary soils to a proper degree of fertility is applied just previous to the Onion crop, it is liable to make the Onions very soft and consequently they will be poor keepers. The quantity of seed required will vary with the soil, the variety to be grown and the grade desired.

Thin seeding gives much larger bulbs than thick seeding. After the first hoeing, weeding must be continued. This is tedious work but it must be carefully and thoroughly done. The operator must work on his knees, astride the row, at the same time stirring the soil around the seedling Onions to destroy any weeds that may have started. In about two weeks they will require another cultivating and possibly another weeding. If the work has been thoroughly done at the proper time the crop will require very little, if any further care until ready to harvest. Have your soil rich, do the work properly and your Onions will thrive and gain strength amazingly.

The best Onion seed is raised from onions that were grown from sets. Sets are small onions grown the previous year from seed sown very thickly (50 to 60 pounds per acre) and gathered when the size of peas. The smaller the better, as they produce the best crop. Set out in the spring they soon form a good large Onion, and also make excellent green Onions quite early. As previously stated the soil must be *very rich*. Do not manure too heavily in the spring or the crop will not be as firm as otherwise and will not keep as well when stored. Where you have any Onions left over from your winter supply they may be set out early and will soon make excellent young Onions to use with early radishes and lettuce.

There are two other kinds of Onions that are not raised from seed; these are the Potato and Top Onions. The former grows in clusters under the soil. These clusters are divided and the sets are planted in the spring and produce large Onions; these large Onions are set out and produce the sets. The latter produce the sets on top of the stalks where seed is produced on the common variety. These sets are planted in the spring and the crop is large Onions, and these with one year's growth produce the sets.

Do not try to grow the Onion on poor, unsuitable soil or in a careless manner. Place the fertilizer on or near the surface *and be cautious of whom you procure your seed*.

The Egytian Perennial, or Winter Onion, is quite hardy and should not be disturbed when once established. They are used for green Onions only and are propogated from the sets which grow on top of the stalks similar to Top Onions. These sets are planted in autumn and covered with stalks or strawy manure; this should be raked off before growth commences in spring. These come *very* early and are sweet and tender. Gather your crop as soon as the tops die down and "cure" them *thoroughly* before you store them for winter. They should be packed in boxes made of lath; these boxes should be 16 inches wide, 24 inches long and 6 inches deep, with a slat nailed on the ends of the bottom to admit air to circulate freely.

Parsley (*Apium petroselinum*).—This useful little plant will grow almost anywhere. It does not require a very rich soil. Sow the seed in drills one foot apart, afterwards thinning the plants to four inches apart. Parsley seed germinates very slowly; therefore previous to sowing soak the seed in warm water for twenty-four hours, or all precau-

tions must be taken to insure success. When sown it
should be covered about half an inch deep with fine soil,
which should be firmed over the seed. Always gather the
large leaves first, and cut off all old ones to encourage
a fresh growth.

Parsley will live through the winter in the garden if protected with leaves; or plant a few roots in a box and place them in a light cellar where they will grow all winter. This herb is used extensively in stuffings, etc.

Parsnip (*Pastinaca sativa*).—This vegetable we find mentioned by Pliny as being brought to Rome from the banks of the Rhine, at the command of the emperor Tiberius, for use on his table, A. D. 14. This delicious vegetable comes to its greatest perfection in a deep, rich and free soil that has been stirred to a depth of 12 inches and having been heavily manured for a previous crop, or the manure used should be thoroughly decayed. Sow in drills 18 inches apart as early in the spring as the soil will permit. When two or three inches high thin to six inches apart. The Parsnip is entirely hardy and improves by being left in the ground through the winter taking only sufficient to the cellar to last while the soil is frozen.

The roots are always best flavored when left where grown; but when raised for market they may be pitted. They can be sold at remunerative prices when the crop in general is frozen in the ground. Be careful to dig the crop clean. Parsnips are also very nutritious food for milch cows and make a very rich and abundant flow of milk.

Peas (*Pisum sativum*).—The Pea is very hardy and will endure considerable cold either above or below the soil and as we all want green Peas as early as possible in the season they should be sown as early as the soil can be prepared in the spring. The earliest varieties are mostly small, round, smooth and more hardy than the wrinkled sorts and the tallest growing not more than three feet high. Of late years some very fine dwarf sweet wrinkled sorts have been added to this class. The late ones are large, mostly wrinkled and formerly were nearly all tall; but very many excellent dwarfs have been added to the list. If the earliest varieties are sown about April 1st they will be ready for use early in June. Those sown a little later will be ready about the Fourth of July.

The large, fine wrinkled varieties are not asy hard as the small round sorts, and if sown very early they should have a dry soil or they are liable to rot. It is well to sow the earliest varieties as early as possible and two or three weeks later make another sowing, a few more early, and some for late use. The very latest varieties will not succeed in this country as they mildew in hot weather.

The Pea does well almost anywhere but it likes a good, though not too rich, soil and deep cultivation. In wet seasons a too rich soil causes the plant to make too much growth which is an injury to the crop; but on the other hand a rich soil which also means a cool soil in a dry season is of the greatest importance. To secure best results sow in moderately rich soil.

Sow Peas in drills not less than two feet apart, and not less than four inches deep, especially the late sowings. The dwarfs which from their small growth are best suited for garden culture may be sown in rows one foot apart and one inch between the seeds. The tall sorts require a support of some kind which should be supplied as soon as the Peas appear. The second sowing previously mentioned comes in nicely and are quite palatable. A row of early and late varieties may be sown side by side at the same time so that the same brush will answer for both. Rake over the rows just as the Peas are coming through the soil. The earliest and latest sowings should be made of dwarf and early varieties.

The thin and deep sowing of Peas tends to make them bushy and prolong the period of bearing. A few may be sprouted in boxes in March and transplanted to the garden when the soil is ready. This will cause them to bear some time before the regular crop. An excellent support for Peas can be made by driving stakes at intervals of 6 or 8 feet in the row and stretching wires on them 6 or 8 inches apart. These may at the end of the season be rolled up and put away for next season. The wires may be secured to the stakes by small staples or by cutting slots slantingly in the stakes so that the wires will lie in them. The stakes should be set firmly in the ground or the weight of the vines and the wind will pull them over. There is nothing better than brush, however, when it is obtainable.

If you use a commercial fertilizer procure one containing a large percent of soluble phosphoric acid. Very little potash is needed where the soil is in fair condition. Strawberries may be set where early Peas were grown. Celery is also a splendid crop to follow early beans and peas.

Peanut (*Arachis hypogaea*).—Although this may not belong to our list of vegetable dietary it may be well to say a few words here concerning its culture. Many a long, dreary winter's evening may be enjoyed and pleasantly passed away by the young folks, and older ones too, by roasting Peanuts or by popping corn; for who is there who does not enjoy Peanuts or popcorn when made into candy or balls.

The Peanut is a low, somewhat creeping annual, a member of the bean family. It is a native of the tropics but thrives in our more northern states. The best variety is said to be the Spanish variety. Being earlier they are less liable to get frosted in the fall. All varieties delight in a rich, sandy loam which contains some lime. Plant as early as possible after danger of frost is past. If you do not have a piece of sandy soil plant on land on which oats were last grown.

Plant in rows two feet apart, dropping the seeds eight inches apart and cover about two inches deep. Destroy all weeds and keep the soil mellow around the plants so that the blossoms may bury themselves. Only the first blooms bear fruit. After blooming, these flowers penetrate the soil several inches where the nuts ripen. A yield of from 80 to 100 bushels per acre is common.

In planting do not break the shell of the nut, as this protects the kernel while germinating and keeps the nut warm while it decays. When ready to harvest pull up and pick off the nuts or "goobers"; shake the dirt from the vines and pile for fodder. When dry the nuts should be sacked and put in a dry place. In roasting use a large iron roasting pan and roast only a few at a time, as fresh nuts are superior to old ones. While roasting stir frequently, being careful not to burn them.

Peppers (*Capsicum*).—This is a genus of plants closely related to the woody nightshade; the fruits are fleshy, of various shapes and sizes and usually of a bright scarlet or orange, more or less pungent and much used for flavoring, both whole and ground. In the latter form it is known as cayenne pepper which is *very* pungent. This vegetable should be found in every garden for mangoes and for other purposes. It is well to remember that the flavor is in inverse ratio to the size of the fruits—the largest being the mildest while the smallest are the most pungent.

Sow in a quite warm hotbed in March and transplant to open ground in May or when danger from cold snaps is past. They should be planted in warm, mellow, rich soil in rows 18 inches apart. They may also be sown in a warm, sunny nook in rich, mellow seedbed in the garden when the nights are warm. Where desired two plants may be set between the hills of cucumbers, melons, etc. As they grow above the vines they are not injured, but benefited by having their roots shaded and the soil kept moist by the broad leaves of the vines. Hen manure is an excellent fertilizer when worked in around the plants and will be found to increase their productiveness and also the quality of the fruits. When gathering the fruits for use pick a few green specimens, as they make a pleasing contrast when mixed with the ripe ones of the red and yellow varieties.

Pumpkin (*Cucurbita*).—No one seems to have been able to trace the origin of either the Pumpkin or squash, but we read of Pumpkin pies being made over 300 years ago, after this recipe: "Cut a hole in the side, take out the seeds and filaments, stuff with a mixture of apples and spices and bake till done."

These take up so much room that they properly belong in the cornfield, but if there is no other place to raise them they may be planted among the sweet corn or potatoes, providing they can be kept far enough from the squashes to prevent their crossing and spoiling the latter. Do not plant until settled weather. Plant in hills 6 feet apart each way and mix 3 or 4 shovelfuls of well rotted manure with the soil of each hill. Plant five or six seeds in each hill. Thin to three plants when about one foot in length. Cultivate and hoe thoroughly until there is danger of injuring the vines. The fruits should be gathered before heavy frosts (leaving the stems to them) being careful not to bruise the Pumpkins, and store in a cool, but frost proof room.

Potatoes, Sweet (*Batatas*).—As these favorites are semi-tropical, they require a long season to mature and must be started in a hotbed. They may be grown in this previous to sowing late cabbage, etc.; or the bed may be constructed in a warm, sunny nook sheltered by a building.

While the sun is warmest about April 1st, rake the bed over thoroughly so as to have the soil fine and of uniform depth. Now lay the seed. If large plants are desired the tubers should be two or three inches apart, carefully pressing them into the soil. When the tubers are laid, cover three inches deep with mellow loam, raking the surface smoothly. If the job is well done the soil will warm up in two or three days, but the temperature must not be allowed to rise above 75° or 80°. The plants may appear in two or three weeks, but this will depend on circumstances. The bed must have air whenever possible. This should be done on warm sunny days by removing the sash for about three hours in the middle of the day. Rake the surface of the bed gently, exercising care that the plants are not injured. Until well up, the bed need not be uncovered every day, and *must* not be on cold, cloudy or stormy days. The plants must be exposed more or less as they grow and the season advances until a week before planting-out time comes, when they should be uncovered night and day to harden them. The beds should be made about six weeks before the plants are needed.

These delicious and universal favorites delight in a sandy loam plowed five or six inches deep and heavily manured. The best manure for this crop is well rotted horse manure. Before planting, or about May 10th, work the soil as fine as possible. Make furrows where the rows are to be, three feet apart. Scatter the manure (compost is best) in these; cover with plow or hoe by drawing the soil from the sides. Level the ridge with a steel rake.

About May 20th set the plants one foot apart on this ridge. Do this just before or after a rain if possible, or water them thoroughly. The time for setting is ruled by the season. The plants will take root in forty-eight hours when all danger from transplanting is over. A long rooted plant is best and should be set to touch the manure or compost. The hoe may be used to good advantage at the first cultivation. When the vines are running nicely they should be lifted up occasionally to prevent their forming new roots. Lay up early and dig before frost has injured them. Cut worms should be caught and made an "example of." A few broods of young chicks scattered through the patch will keep down the bugs. Sweet Potatoes may be dug as soon as large enough and the crop must be harvested before frost.

The old plan of raising this gem of crops, though almost out of date now is still one of the best and is certain and cheap. The plan was to make a hog or cow yard on a spot suited to the growth of the "Potato," and the crop grown on this. Here you can raise the largest and finest tubers you ever saw. This is also a splendid spot for turnips.

After digging allow the tubers to dry, then place in a warm, dry place in sand or road dust gathered in summer.

Potatoes (*Solanum tuberosum*).—The Potato is a native of this country and was first discovered by Sir Walter Raleigh in 1586 in Virginia and has become one of the most valuable products of the soil and is in universal use throughout the entire civilized world.

The Potato, like all robust growing vegetables, can be

grown with varying success on soils of varying composition and in all stages of fertility, but a sandy loam is best suited to their growth. Clover sod is excellent and will produce good crops when well worked and properly fertilized. Heavy soils are liable to produce a sickly, diseased crop and the flavor is also inferior to those raised on a light, dry soil. An old pasture field in good fertility will produce splendid crops, as the decaying sod fills the place of manure the first season. But as all grow Potatoes and must use such soil as we have, whether it is suitable or not, we must make as much as possible out of our land and circumstances.

The manure should be broadcasted on the surface and either plowed or harrowed in. The latter is sometimes preferable, especially if the manure is thoroughly decayed. If the soil is in good fertility very little fertilizing will be required. In highly enriched soil the crop will be more liable to disease than in cases where the soil is naturally good. Fresh manure often produces a rough, scabby crop of tubers. The best fertilizers are those of a dry or absorbent nature, bone dust, lime, plaster, superphosphate of lime, etc. In wet localities these are quite beneficial as they not only promote growth but are a preventive against disease. A good dressing of wood ashes is good even on rich soil.

When the main crop is to be grown in the garden, plant as early as the soil is in good working condition and harvest as soon as ripe. In so doing the soil may be used for turnips, late cabbage, etc., (in this case seed of some early heading variety should be sown) or other second crop vegetable. In the garden the rows need not be more than 2½ feet apart and the hills 18 inches and if the soil is mellow as it should be, about 6 inches deep; while if the soil is hard, wet clay, not more than 4 inches. Cut the "sets" with two or three eyes to each. It is also a good plan to cut the seed a few days before needed, so that the cuts will heal over before planting. By so doing the sets will not be so liable to decay, and, too, they will come up sooner. I would not under any circumstances recommend the use of small, whole potatoes for seed as the "eyes" are small. This means weak, spindling tops and as a strong, healthy vine is as essential to the tubers as healthy lungs or hearts are to our good health we may be excused for saying, "no top, no tater." Then again we do not use the nubbins of corn or light wheat or oats for seed, and why use small Potatoes?

The first crop planted should be of some extra early variety. While as a rule these are not good yielders, they fill the vacancy between the old and new crop. The main crop should be of some of the more robust-growing later-maturing varieties. After planting keep the soil mellow by giving it a light harrowing as soon as the potatoes are well sprouted. This is quite important, especially if the soil is inclined to be hard, as it gives the plants a chance to get through and also to get a "start in life" and at the same time destroys a crop of weeds. *Do not harrow after they have come up.* As soon as the tops show enough to follow the rows start the cultivator or hoe and loosen the soil close to the plants and draw a little mellow soil up to them. They may even be slightly covered without injuring them. This not only kills another crop of weeds, but also protects the Potatoes from the ravages of the potato bug.

For planting, select medium sized tubers of the form characteristic of the variety. By planting at the depth given, very little hilling will be necessary. Low, flat ridges are the best, as they retain the moisture and keep the soil cool, which is so much needed from the time cultivation has ceased until the crop has matured, which is necessary to good yields; while high, abrupt hills shed off the rain too readily, leaving the roots dry, which is detrimental to the crop.

To test the quality of the Potato it should be eaten without the addition of any seasoning and will be found best as soon as cooked. New varieties are originated by sowing the seed from the "seed balls," which is saved as is tomato seed and sown in fine, rich soil and carefully cultivated. The crops will be of various forms and colors and occasionally a variety of real merit and worth will be obtained; but this is not an every-day occurrence.

Cultivate your crop thoroughly and ridge up just before the plants come into bloom. Keep the bugs in check by the methods given in the chapter on Injurious Insects, and success will be yours. Pull all large weeds out of the ridges to give the patch a tidy appearance and to prevent their re-seeding the ground. For myself there is no crop on the farm that gives more pride than a large crop of nice, large, smooth Potatoes. The crop should be harvested as soon as the tops have matured and spread where they will be dry and cool until they have gone through the "sweat."

When storing for winter it is a good idea to sort them, placing each grade by itself, storing those which you wish to keep in a cool, dry and dark place. The small ones make splendid feed for little pigs when boiled and mashed and mixed with their food. Handle the tubers carefully when sorting so as not to bruise them or they will decay. Nicely sorted Potatoes give a much finer appearance than a "mixed lot" and are much nicer to cook and also give a "well set" appearance to any table. The tubers may be buried or pitted in the garden as are beets, carrots, etc., but there is no place better suited to their storage than a well ventilated cellar.

Radish (*Raphanus sativus*).—A book entitled "The Radish" was written before the time of Christ. The ancient Greeks used to offer turnips, beets and radishes in their oblations to Apollo. The first was offered in dishes of lead, the second in silver and the third in "vessels of beaten gold."

To obtain good, crisp, sweet eating Radishes they must be grown quickly. The most suitable soil is one moderately light, and which has been fairly manured for some previous crop. Sowings should be made throughout the summer so as to always have a supply. Beautiful, crisp Radishes may be had throughout the winter by sowing some of the winter varieties in August.

For an early crop seed should be sown in the hot bed in drills five or six inches apart and half an inch deep. Give but little heat and plenty of air. For an early crop outside sow on a south border under the shelter of a fence or building if possible. A supply of fresh, sandy loam from the woods is better than manure for the Radish crop. As soon as the first leaves appear sprinkle with ashes or soot (when dry) to save them from the little black flea beetle.

The winter varieties should be sown in July or early in August when they will make fine large roots for winter use and will be greatly relished. They should be dug before severe freezing weather and pitted out of doors or buried in earth in a cool cellar. They will then keep crisp all winter. An hour before using place in cold water. The heart leaves of the Radish should be eaten along with the Radish to aid in digesting the Radish itself. The young seed leaves may be used as a salad while the green seed pods, especially of *R. Caudatus*, make excellent pickles.

Radishes may be sown thinly along with carrots, beets, etc, to good advantage.

Rhubarb or Pie-Plant (*Rheum hybridum*).—This vegetable, familiarly known as Pie-Plant, is cultivated for its leaf stalks, which are used for pies and tarts. No private garden large or small should be without its bed of Rhubarb, as it comes very early and is quite healthful.

It succeeds best in a deep, somewhat retentive soil. The richer the soil and the deeper stirred the better. Sow the seed in drills six inches apart and an inch deep and thin the plants to six inches apart. The soil should be rich and mellow, when strong plants will be obtained in one season, but very little cutting should be done until the third year. In the fall after sowing transplant the young plants into highly manured soil three feet each way and give a dressing of coarse manure every fall. Do not allow the plants to exhaust themselves by running to seed. Plants set out in rich soil in the spring are in fine condition the second season.

To do the best Rhubarb must be divided and reset every few years. The bed, if prepared with care, will stand several years if the soil selected is a rich, deep loam that is mellow and not subject to injury by drought. As it is a gross feeder the soil can scarcely be made too rich; it should be plowed deeply and the subsoil should also be broken, in all to the depth of 15 to 18 inches. The planting is best done in April or November. If done in the fall some of the heads will winter-kill and will need replanting. The soil should be put in as good order as for corn. The sets are then set in rows at the distance given and covered two inches deep, one set in a place, with fine soil. Care should be taken that the sets do not become withered from exposure to sun or wind.

The cultivation the first year is simply frequent tillage or hoeing to destroy the weeds. The stalks should be allowed to grow, so as to establish the roots. The second season the stalks will be ready to gather but you must cut sparingly until the third season. For three or four seasons the crop will be in perfection. Give the bed a very heavy dressing of manure every fall after the frost has killed the leaves. It will be necessary to cultivate two or three times in the spring to destroy the weeds that may appear.

In the spring two or three weeks before the frost has gone, cover a few of the roots with barrels and bank these with a heap of horse manure and in a short time you will have tender and delicious Pie-plant in abundance. Or another way is to dig up some well grown roots in November, storing them in a cool place until February, when they may be taken out and placed in the cellar and covered with a few inches of loam. No light, but a temperature of 60° is all that is necessary, except that the roots will need an abundance of water as they come into growth. Pull the stalks when about a foot long.

The forced roots are worthless for future use and are thrown away. To have a supply of nice juicy stalks for

fall use keep the old ones pulled and cultivate in August
and growth will again commence. Rhubarb will thrive
under almost any treatment when the soil is moist, but not
wet.

Sage (*Salvia officinallis*).—As this herb is an universal
favorite it may be well to give the reader a few hints as to
its culture.

Sow the seed in drills one foot apart and cover about an
inch deep with very fine soil. This should be done in the
spring when the soil has become warm. When the plants
have grown a few inches in height set them in rows eighteen
inches apart each way. Cultivate several times during the
season.

Sage is quite hardy and if the soil is not wet it will remain in the garden all winter, but it is best to give some
protection, however. In the spring take up the plants,
separate the roots and reset them.

Some gardeners treat this crop as an annual where it is
grown on a large scale by sowing the seed in the spring,
gathering the leaves before frost and then plowing the plants
under. I think, however, for garden use it is best to follow
the directions given, cutting the stems or plucking the
leaves just before the plants bloom, spreading them in the
shade to dry. If seed is desired allow some of the best
plants to ripen. When ripe the seed is black and when it
reaches that condition the stems bearing it should be cut
and dried. Holt's Mammoth is the best and is grown from
plants (that is, by layering) only.

Plants of either variety may be grown by laying down
some of the branches and covering them with soil. If
grown at home you are sure of it being fresh; while if obtained at the grocery it is liable to be old and its flavor gone
or almost so, making it of little value.

Salsify (*Tragopogon porrifolius*).—This is one of the most
delicious and healthful of vegetables and should be more
generally grown for winter use, when the supply of really
good vegetables is so scarce. It prefers a fairly good,
light soil; but to have well-shaped, clean and straight roots
use thoroughly decayed manured thoroughly mixed with
the soil which should be stirred to a good depth. Soil
made rich for some previous crop is best suited to its growth,
as coarse manure would surely cause the roots to grow uneven and ill-shaped.

Prepare the soil thoroughly and sow as early as the soil
can be worked. It should be sown quite deeply, about two

inches, giving the culture recommended for the parsnip. The rows should be about one foot apart. When ready thin to six inches apart. The roots are perfectly hardy and may remain where grown all winter but must be dug early before growth commences, as the quality deteriorates rapidly after that; or they may be taken up and stored in a pit as are beets, carrots, etc.

Salsify has a grassy top and a long, white, tapering root which closely resembles a parsnip, while it closely assimulates to the taste and flavor of the oyster, when properly prepared, for which it is sometimes used as a substitute—hence its name, Oyster plant. The roots are either boiled or mashed and made into fritters, in which form they are delicious, and in fact a great luxury.

Spinach (*Spinacca oleracea*).—Spinach thrives in any good garden soil but the richer the soil the more succulent will be the leaves.

For a succession of this crop sowings of the round leafed sorts should be made from early spring to June. For winter use seed of the hardy varieties may be sown in August or September, in rich but well drained soil in rows one foot apart, and when about one inch wide the plants should be thinned to four inches apart. On the approach of winter the plants should be protected by straw, leaves or litter in the north. Seed of the ordinary sorts should be sown in drills one foot apart and one inch deep. Thin as above and cut the plants while young and tender.

Spinach makes a most delicious dish and cooks a beautiful green, is very hardy and extremely wholesome and palatable. All Spinach should be cut before hot weather or it will be tough and stringy. In the southern states it needs no protection but will continue to grow most of the winter. The New Zealand variety (*Tetragonia expansa*) supplies the place of the ordinary varieties during the summer months. Sow in May where the plants are to grow and they will yield abundantly all summer, requiring but very little attention.

Squash (*Cucurbita ovifera*).—As stated in pumpkin culture the Squash has been known for centuries. These, like the other members of the *Cucurbita* family, are of tropical origin; therefore it is useless to plant them before the soil is warm and all danger of frost or cold nights is past. And as they make a very rapid growth there is no necessity of getting the seed into the ground so early as to endanger the crop. Squashes are strong feeders and must have a rich soil. It is most economical to manure in the hill as for melons, pumpkins, etc. Hen manure makes an excellent fertilizer for Squashes.

For the "bush" varieties make the hills three feet apart, while for the "running" varieties they should be twice this distance. The former are used while young and tender, while the latter when thoroughly ripened will usually keep till spring, when the bush varieties are again ready. When properly matured the winter varieties are dry and sweet, while if not thoroughly ripened they are watery and lack sweetness and richness and will not keep through the winter. These, like melons, should be encouraged to make a strong growth early in the season.

The shell of the Hubbard and some others when ripe is as hard as the shell of a cocoanut. When ready for use the skin of the summer varieties may be cut with the nail without difficulty, while if any push is required they are too old for use, and will be tough and stringy when cooked. The winter varieties in some sections are more difficult to raise as they are subject to the attacks of the borer which cuts them off under the surface, and for this reason the plants should not be thinned before they are a foot long to insure against loss.

The Squashes should be gathered before any hard frosts, and should be stored in a cool, airy room where they will usually keep well till late in the spring. All varieties should be sown as early as possible after the soil becomes sufficiently warm. A few hills may be sown earlier and covered with straw if there is any danger of J. Frost nipping the tender plants. The land should be rich; the richer the better, and should contain sufficient sand to make it warm and light. A southern slope is best for all vine crops so they can secure the warm rays of the sun. Cultivate the space between the rows as well as around the hills until the vines cover the surface. Watch for and destroy the bugs and cultivate quite shallow around the plants. I have often grown good crops when planted with early potatoes, thus economizing space.

Some of the winter varieties are equally good for summer use if they are used while quite young. If these are planted the one sowing will do for both seasons. When gathering the crop care must be taken not to break the stem from those intended for winter use, as the slightest injury will increase the liability to decay.

Turnip (*Brassica Rapa*).—Every garden should contain a supply of these throughout the season. A rich, mellow

72   THE FARMER'S GARDEN

soil with a fair amount of moisture is most suitable for growing sweet, crisp and tender turnips, but any soil well stirred and manured will grow them well. This splendid vegetable is very easily affected in flavor as well as form by weather, soil, culture, etc.

A very good crop may be grown on soil previously occupied by early potatoes or any early crop. After digging the potatoes, level and firm the soil by rolling or otherwise to retain the moisture and sow the seed either broadcast or in drills. I would prefer to drill them as they can then be cultivated which will greatly hasten their maturity. Getting

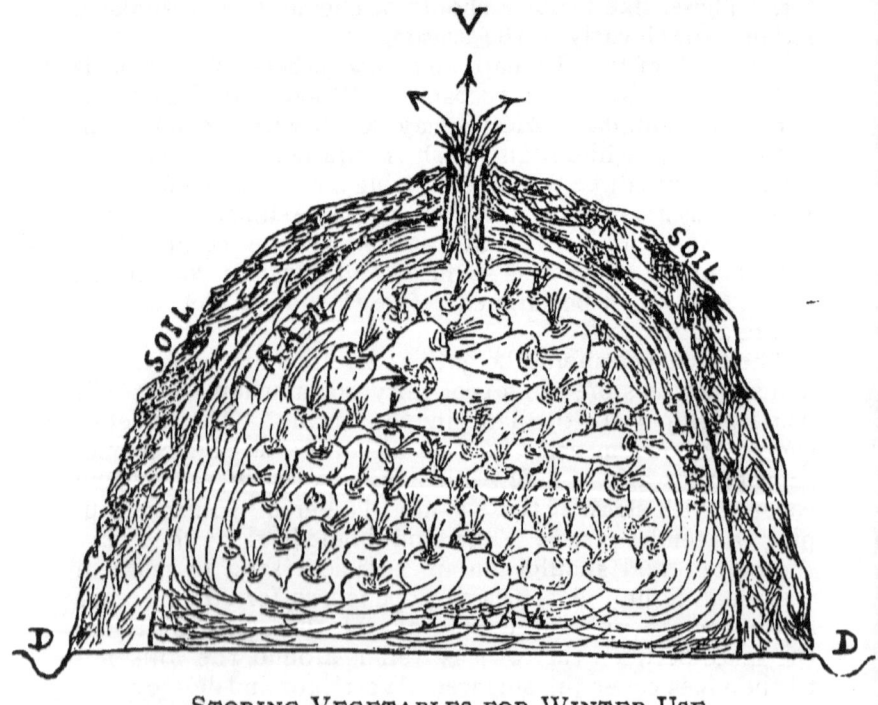

STORING VEGETABLES FOR WINTER USE.

The above illustration really belongs in the general intoductory, pages 5 to 24, but was by mistake omitted.

DIRECTIONS—Select a spot that is high and dry, and place straw to the depth of 6 or 8 inches on the ground. Pile the vegetables, (beets, carrots, turnips, potatoes, etc.), on this, putting from 5 to 20 bushels in a pile, heaping them up cone shape. Now cover them with straw or marsh hay. This may be omitted (except in case of potatoes), but is of great advantage in keeping the vegetables clean and as a protection against frost. On this straw a small drain tile should be set to serve as a ventilator. Soil should now be thrown on the straw and around the tile (packing it firmly so as to prevent the heavy rains and melting snows from soaking in), and to a sufficient depth to prevent the freezing of the contents of the pit —from 6 inches to 1 foot is usually sufficient, according to your locality. On the approach of severe weather the tile should be filled with straw and a board laid on top to exclude frosts. When severe weather sets in cover the mound with corn stalks or straw as a further precaution, and you can enjoy vegetables all winter as fresh and crisp as when first dug. Rats and mice are very destructive to vegetables thus stored and must be guarded against.

the soil into a finely prepared state before sowing is of the greatest importance. For an early crop sow in April, while for a succession of summer and autumn crops make an occasional sowing up to the end of July. For winter use sow in August or September.

Turnips to be of fine quality must be grown quickly; therefore sow in drills twelve to fifteen inches apart, thinning them to eight inches apart. Keep free from weeds while small by giving them an occasional cultivating which will also greatly facilitate their growth.

Turnips may be preserved until spring by cutting off the tops about an inch from the bulb and storing in the cellar or cool shed and covering them with dry sand; or they may be pitted in the garden like other roots. Or store them in barrels along the cellar wall and cover with sand or turf, or they may be piled on the cellar floor and covered with straw eight or ten inches deep.

History proves that Turnips were in use as a garden vegetable before the christian era. Where we have long winters the family gardener should always try to keep the table well supplied with vegetables. If you have a dark corner in your green house or a cellar that excludes frost; a few inches of sand or soil may be placed on the floor; on this Turnips may be placed close together and gently pressed into it, after which give them a watering and close them up. In a short time your heart will be gladdened by beautiful blanched leaf stalks. These should be cut and tied in bunches as is asparagus and cooked in a similar manner; they will then be pronounced "excellent." In this way you can have a very delicious vegetable all winter by planting at intervals.

Tomato (*Lycopersicum esculentum*).—The growth of this delicious vegetable has progressed by "leaps and bounds" and will continue to advance in public estimation. Only a few years ago when grandmother was a girl they were known as "love apples" and considered as being poisonous, being grown as a curiosity, their bright scarlet fruits being considered very attractive. It is a mistake to suppose that there is any difficulty in its cultivation, as it may be successfully grown in any well kept garden.

Sow the seed in hot bed or box placed in a sunny window where the temperature does not fall below 60°, about the first of March or ten weeks before the last frost is expected, in rows about five inches apart and one-half inch deep. When the plants are about two inches high transplant in boxes or hot beds, setting them about four inches apart each way, in same temperature; or they may be set in small pots one plant to each pot and set them in the hot bed; by this method the plants are rendered more stocky and branching. Give the plants plenty of air on pleasant days to prevent their becoming "drawn" and to make them bushy.

Transplant to the open ground as soon as all danger from frost is past, in hills 3x3 feet apart for an early crop, on a light soil with a dry subsoil, having previously mixed a shovelful of thoroughly decayed manure with the soil. On heavy soil not suited to an early crop the plants should be set 4x4 feet apart. In transplanting dig a hole large enough to hold the roots without much crowding, set the plant and pour water into the hole and gently fill up the hole with mellow soil, shading the plants from the sun for a day or two until they become established. These and egg plants are the second choice of the potato bug, the "old fashioned" one especially. To hasten the maturity of the first fruits, pinch out the tips of the vines and all the secondary shoots that appear above the flowers. The tomato may also be grown in the green house by following the above rules. While some train their plants to a single vine others prefer a small ladder, while others allow them to take the course provided by nature, i. e., that of lying on the ground.

There seems to be no preventative for the rot which quite often attacks the tomato. As is well known, if the chickens can get into the garden they will play havoc with the crop. Watch for the large tomato worm, for they will destroy your vines if they themselves are not killed. These worms make a peculiar sound when disturbed and are said to be poisonous.

There is another species of the tomato plant known as the Strawberry, Husk or Ground Cherry tomato, (*Alkekengi*) which grows enclosed in a husk, similar to the ground cherry, and are cultivated similar to the Tomato proper. The fruits are about the size of the hickory nut, and of a bright golden yellow color. When used as fruit for dessert, in pies or preserves they are simply grand.

By picking all ripe fruit from tomato vines the yield will be greatly increased and the period of bearing greatly lengthened. All rotten specimens should also be gathered. In very rich garden soil tomatoes often make such a rank growth of vine as to shade and blight the blossoms. To prevent this thin out the branches so as to admit sun and air to penetrate, or try the Tree tomato tied to a single stake. Tomatoes are best when used fresh from the vine. A slight check received while the plants are small will materially lessen the crop.

Quantity of Seed Required

to produce a given number of plants and to sow an acre of ground. Good seeds should always be sown regardless of price. Poor seeds are dear even as a gift.

Names of Seeds and Number of Plants.   Amount Per Acre

Artichoke, 1 ounce to 600 plants,......................6 ounces
Asparagus, 1 ounce to 1500 plants, to transplant,...2 pounds
Barley,..2½ bushels
Beans, Dwarf, 1 pint to 1 quart to 100 feet,.. 1 to 2 bushels
Beans, Pole, large, 1 quart to 100 hills,...............¾ bushel
Beans, Pole, small, 1 quart to 200 hills,...............1½ peck
Beet, garden, 1 ounce to 100 feet of drill, in rows 3 feet apart,..4 pounds
Beet, Mangel, 1 ounce to 100 feet,...............6 to 8 pounds
Brocoli, 1 oz to 9000 plants,..........................1½ ounces
Brussels Sprouts, 1 ounce to 12000 plants,.............1 ounce
Buckwheat,...½ bushel
Cabbage, 1 ounce to 6000 plants,........................2 ounces
Carrot, 1 ounce to 200 feet of drill,...............3 to 4 pounds
Cauliflower, 1 ounce to 7000 to 9000 plants,....1 to ½ ounces
Celery, 1 ounce to 35000 to 70000,if sown thinly, 2 ounces
Clover, White and Alsace,...............................6 pounds
Clover, Lucerne, L. Red and Crimson Trefoil,......8 pounds
Clover, Medium,...10 pounds
Collards, 1 ounce to 9500 plants, to transplant,...... 2 ounces
Corn, Broom,..10 pounds
Corn, Pop, (Rice),.. 2 quarts
Corn, Sweet, 1 pint to 100 hills, 300 feet of row, ...8 to 10 quarts
Corn, Field,...8 to 10 quarts
Cress, Fine Curled, 1 ounce to 12000 plants, Water Cress, 1 ounce to 160000 plants, Upland Cress 1 ounce to 80000 plants,............................12 pounds
Cucumbers, 1 ounce to 50 hills, in hills 3x3 feet, 3 pounds
Egg Plant, 1 ounce to 6000 plants, 4000 per acre,.¾ ounce
Endive, 1 ounce to 100 feet, in rows 3 feet apart,.. 3 pounds
Flax, sown broadcast, ...½ bushel
Garlic, 1 pound to 10 feet,...
Gourds, 1 ounce to 25 hills,..
Grass, Kentucky Blue,...................................2 bushels
Grass, English Blue, ...1 bushel
Grass, Hungarian Millet,.........................½ to 1 bushel
Grass, Lawn, Mixed,.............................3 to 4 bushels
Grass, Orchard, Perennial Rye, Red Top, Fowl ....
Grass, Meadow and Woods Meadow,................2 bushels

Grass, Redtop, Fancy,............................8 to 10 pounds
Grass, Timothy,...¼ bushel
Hemp,..½ bushel
Kale or Borecole, 1 ounce to 9000 plants,............2 ounces
Kohl Rabi, 1 ounce to 6000 plants, in row 3 feet
    apart,..4 pounds
Leek, 1 ounce to 9000 plants, 100 feet of drill......4 pounds
Lettuce, 1 ounce to 1200 ft., 30000 plants...........3 pounds
Martynia, 1 ounce to 100 plants, ...5 pounds
Melon, Musk, 1 ounce to 50 hills, in hills 4x4 ft. 3 pounds
Melon, Water, 2 ounces to 50 hills,.....................3 pounds
Mustard, varies greatly,..
Nasturtium, 1 ounce to 200 feet,.....................15 pounds
Oats, ...2 bushels
Okra, 1 ounce to 50 feet or 50 hills,................. 8 pounds
Onion, Seed, for large bulbs, 1 ounce to 200 feet..4 pounds
Onion, Seed for sets,..............................50 to 60 pounds
Onion Sets, vary greatly according to size, 1 quart
    to 40 to 100 feet,...............................8 to 10 bushels
Parsnips, 1 ounce to 200 feet,......................3 to 4 pounds
Parsley, 1 ounce to 200 feet, 15000 plants,..........4 pounds
Peas, Early, 1 quart to 125 feet, ...2½ bushels
Peas, Late, 1 quart to 200 feet,......................2½ bushels
Pepper, about 1 ounce to 5000 to 9000 plants, 10000
    plants per acre,............................... 1 to 1½ ounces
Potatoes,...8 to 12 bushels
Pumpkin, 1 pound to 300 hills,....................3 to 5 pounds
Radish, 1 ounce to 100 feet, on an average,........14 pounds
Rhubarb, 1 ounce to 2000 plants,.....................2½ ounces
Rye,..1½ bushels
Salsify, 1 ounce to 100 feet,..............................8 pounds
Spinach, 1½ ounces to 100 feet, in drills, ...8 pounds
Squash, Summer, 2 ounces to 50 hills,................3 pounds
Squash, Winter, 2 ounces to 25 hills,..................4 pounds
Tomato, 1 ounce to 10000 plants, sown thinly,......2 ounces
Tobacco, 1 ounce to 2500 plants,.......................3 ounces
Turnips, 1 ounce to 200 feet of drill, broadcast 1
    pound, in drills, ...2 to 3 pounds
Tares or Vetches,...2½ bushels
Wheat,..1½ to 2 bushels

  The above is based on seeds of first class quality.

Number of Trees, Plant or Shrubs.

After giving the foregoing we give the following table so that you can easily ascertain the number of trees, plants or shrubs required to plant any given space at almost any distance:

Distance apart	No. of plants per acre
3 inches by 3 inches	696,960
4 " " 4 "	392,040
6 " " 6 "	174,240
9 " " 9 "	77,440
1 foot by 6 inches	87,126
1 " " 1 foot	43,560
1½ feet by 1½ feet	19,360
2 " " 6 inches	21,792
2 " " 1 foot	10,896
2½ " " 2½ feet	6,960
3 " " 6 inches	29,040
3 " " 1 foot	14,520
3 " " 2 feet	7,260
3 " " 3 "	4,840
3½ " " 3½ feet	3,555
4 " " 6 inches	21,780
4 " " 1 foot	10,890
4 " " 2 feet	5,445
4 " " 3 "	3,630
4 " " 4 "	2,722
4½ " " 4½ feet	2,151
5 " " 6 inches	17,424
5 " " 1 foot	8,712
5 " " 2 feet	4,356
5 " " 3 "	2,904
5 " " 4 "	2,178
5 " " 5 "	1,742
5½ " " 5½ feet	1,440
6 " " 6 "	1,210
6½ " " 6½ "	1,031
7 " " 7 "	888
8 " " 8 "	680
9 " " 9 "	537
10 " " 10 "	435
11 " " 11 "	360
12 " " 12 "	302
13 " " 13 "	257
14 " " 14 "	222
15 " " 15 "	193
16 " " 16 "	170

17 feet by	17 feet	....	150
18 " "	18 "	....	134
19 " "	19 "	....	120
20 " "	20 "	....	108
25 " "	25 "	....	69
30 " "	30 "	....	48
33 " "	33 "	....	40
40 " "	40 "	....	27
50 " "	50 "	....	17
60 " "	60 "	....	12
66 " "	66 "	....	10

By reference to this table and the preceding one it is a very simple matter to calculate just how much seed or the number of plants will be required to plant a given space. Of course it is impossible to tell to a certainty just how many plants a given amount of seed will produce, as much depends on the quality of the seed used; but good seed will, with proper care, give about the number stated. It is always a good plan to test your seeds as to their vitality, purity, etc. The following is a good way: Place 100 seeds in a small box of earth or sand; keep at a temperature about the same as they would be if in the open ground or hotbed as the case might be. If good they will soon germinate. The number germinating will indicate the percentage good. Plant accordingly. Age has a marked effect on the vitality of seeds. Fresh seeds are always to be desired, as they germinate more quickly. It is said, however, that the older cabbage seed is, not to have lost its vitality, the better; while the older vine seeds are, the thicker will be the flesh. In a work of this nature we do not have space to enter into the details of this, but a great deal may be learned by experimenting and noticing the effects of such experiments. As to how long seeds will retain their vitality is uncertain as so much depends on the state of their maturity when harvested, and the way in which they were afterwards cared for. For examining seeds as to purity, scatter them on a piece of black card board when the foreign grains may be readily observed.

SMALL FRUITS.

Every garden large or small should produce sufficient small fruits for at least home requirements, for the following reasons: First, because they materially lessen the expense of keeping up the table; second, because they are healthy and nutritious diet; and third, because no garden is complete without them. By judicious selection and careful planting you may have an abundance of ripe, delicious berries from June 1st to October 1st; strawberries for June, raspberries for July, blackberries for August, and grapes for September and October.

It is a very common sight in nearly all gardens to see the fruit bushes of all kinds planted along the fences, causing not only a loss of half of the fruit, as it can only be borne on one side of the bushes, but causing much unnecessary labor in keeping the soil worked and unless cultivated frequently the plot soon becomes an unpenetrable jungle of weeds and briers and will be pronounced "no good."

The hardiness of a plant is not determined by the severity of the weather so much as by its ability to stand the alternate freezing and thawing in close succession. For the reason just given I would prefer to have the small fruit plot on the north side of the garden, especially if it is the highest and if there is some kind of a wind-break to protect the bushes, as this will cause the snow to drift around them and be longer about them, making a natural protection, while the slope of the soil will cause the surface water to drain away quickly, so that it will not stand around the plants and damage them by freezing about the crowns. The most suitable soil in which to grow small fruits is a deep rich loam well drained. Never under any circumstances use weak plants or plants that are infected in any way, or disappointment is sure to be your reward.

Strawberry (*Fragaria virginiana*).—As Strawberries are the first to mature their delicious fruits, we will first consider their culture. The first thing to do is to start right; and that means to select a good clean plot of ground, prepare it thoroughly and set out the plants. Strawberries will thrive on any good soil that will produce good garden crops or a good crop of corn. Prepare your soil as early in the spring as circumstances will permit by plowing deep, thoroughly pulverizing, heavily manuring and well draining. There are so many ways of culture that it is difficult to say which is best. For garden culture, set the plants two feet each way and let one runner grow between each plant one way and keep off all other runners. This would cause the plants to be one foot apart in the rows until the first of September when only the surface should be cultivated, so as to destroy what few weeds would grow after this, as the plants now begin to produce numerous lateral runners, which if disturbed would injure the crop. For large plump berries keep the plants in hills.

Although some plant in August or September, which will answer in many cases, I would recommend spring planting. But if one has good potted plants and is careful in planting he may have a crop the following season. These potted plants are obtained by filling small pots with rich soil and sinking them up to the brim in the earth near the best plants in July, when vigorously throwing out runners; and press the runners where the plant is forming down into the soil of the pot, placing a small clod or stone to hold it in place. Nip off the end of the runner beyond the plant. As soon as the roots fill the pot cut the runner from the parent plant and turn the new plant out and plant with all the soil clinging to the roots.

When planting, draw a line and make the hole with a trowel or spade. Take the plant in the left hand, spread the roots fan shaped in the hole; press the soil to the roots and the work is done. Be sure your plants have good roots. Do not cover the crown of the plant or it will die. Never allow the plants to wilt while setting. Keep them wet and the soil will adhere to them and cause them to grow quickly. A good plan is to keep the plants in a bucket with the roots in water. If the roots are long cut off about one-third of their length. This will cause them to produce a multitude of new roots which is very beneficial. Commence to stir the soil early in the season before the weeds begin to grow, keeping the soil clean and mellow throughout the season. Pinch off all blossoms as soon as they appear for if left on they will fruit and cause many of the plants to die and weaken all of them.

When the ground freezes late in the fall so that it will hold your weight, cover the plants with straw, leaves or strawy manure. Do not cover until the soil is frozen hard nor so deep as to smother the plants, and remove covering before the plants start in the spring. This mulching not only protects the plants from the cold, from heaving out of the ground by the alternate freezing and thawing, but also keeps the fruit clean and the soil clean and in fine condition throughout the fruiting season. When strawberries require washing they lose a considerable part of their flavor.

Where economy is necessary stick to the old favorites. Don't experiment with high priced, highly lauded varieties more than on a small scale. Leave experiments to those who have money to spare. In selecting varieties be content with such varieties as your neighbor succeeds with as a great many of the new ones are worthless and dear as a gift.

The strawberry bed cannot be kept in one place as it must be renewed quite frequently. A very satisfactory plan is to plant a new bed each year, plowing up the old one as soon as done bearing. This is an excellent spot on which to raise some splendid turnips or late cucumbers. Economy is wealth, and wealth is what we all want.

There are three varieties of Strawberry plants as distinguished by their sex. These are Staminate, Pistilate and Hermaphrodite. The first is purely male, the second purely female, while the third is a union of both sexes. The former never bears but is used to fertilize the pistilates; while the latter or hermaphrodites are bi-sexual and produce of themselves. The pistilate varieties include some of our most productive varieties when planted near those of a perfect flowering character. Be sure to use well rotted manure freely.

Raspberry.—This splendid fruit is next in season to the strawberry, and is not only delicious but very healthful and should have a place in every garden. The soil best adapted to their growth is a rich gravelly loam, not too rich, but should be in good condition. Where they are planted in a too rich soil they are apt to grow too rank and be easily killed by the severe winter weather.

Raspberries are of two classes—Antwerps and Black caps. The first propagates itself from "suckers" like the blackberry, while the latter increases from "tips" which grow in the latter part of the season from the branches which bend over and take root. If these fail to root naturally they should be buried in August or September where a supply is desired. Treat all surplus ones like weeds. It is best to plant Antwerps in rather thin soil and manure in the hills, using well rotted manure. Black caps (*Rubus occidentalis*) require richer soil.

Make the rows five feet apart and set the plants about three feet apart in the rows and about three inches deep; spread the roots in every direction, then cover the roots with fine soil. If planted in the autumn, make a mound of earth over each hill to prevent the water from standing around the crowns, and to prevent the frost from heaving them out. In the spring draw it away. Care should be taken not to break the tender germ at the root of the plant when planting; for if broken off it will take considerable time to start another if it starts at all. Cultivate thoroughly, destroying every weed if you expect success. When the plants have attained one foot in height nip off the tip of the plant; this will cause them to branch and become stocky. All branches should be treated in a similar manner, and the second year trim all stems to within one foot of the main stalk. When this is not attended to the plants are liable to over bear and be almost useless afterwards. The second season after planting they will produce a few berries. Cultivate the same as first year.

When the plants are about two feet high nip out the tips of the plants and when the side shoots are of same length they should be treated in like manner. As soon as the fruiting season is over, cut out the old growth (that is that which has just borne) so as to give the new growth plenty of space; trim back side branches in the spring. When trimmed in this manner stakes are not necessary. After the first year cultivation should be shallow so as to not injure the roots and cause them to throw up numerous sprouts. Treat all suckers as weeds, cutting them off with a sharp hoe just underneath the surface, but not deep enough to injure the roots. Allow about three stalks to come up in each hill every year.

Clean out the bushes thoroughly and burn all trimmings. It is not safe to cultivate after July as they will grow too late and consequently winter kill. Raspberry plantations arrive at perfection the third year after their formation, and if properly cared for will produce for a long time. As a rule it is not advisable, however, to retain them for more than seven or eight years; and whenever there is a falling off in yield it is a pretty good sign that the plot should be renewed.

The Blackberry.—This delicious favorite follows the raspberry, and as there is certainly none more wholesome everyone should raise at least sufficient for home use. There are, however, a great many people who depend on the fence corners for a supply. As these are often of very inferior quality, and are not always to be had, everyone should have a generous supply for daily use, and should have them where they can be readily obtained, for there is no fruit more easily grown.

Select a plot of ground not very moist or rich. If elevated, so much the better, as they are not so liable to winter kill. Moderately rich soil of a clayey or gravelly nature seems to suit the Blackberry, for if the soil is very rich they make too much wood and are not so productive. Plant as early in the spring as possible. Make furrows where the rows are to be and spread thoroughly rotted manure or compost in these. This will give the young plants a good start, causing the roots to grow along the row instead of spreading out. Make the rows six feet apart and three feet between the plants. The space between the rows may be occupied by corn, potatoes, etc.

Cultivate shallow but thoroughly, being careful not to injure the roots and never take plants from a bearing plantation. The cultivation for the first season is the same as that given for raspberries. In the second as well as succeeding seasons nip off the tips when the plants attain a growth of four or five feet. If they are left to grow their entire length they will not bear so well and, too, they will bend over and interfere with the future care of the plantation. Use the hoe on every sucker as though it was a weed, except those that are required for the future crop. Keep these in a direct row not more than eighteen inches apart.

As soon as the fruiting season is over cut out the canes that have borne fruit, as they are of no further use. Mulch with corn stalks, dry manure, leaves, or anything that will answer the purpose. This not only prevents evaporation which is detrimental to the crop, but as it decays it will furnish a good dressing of manure. In *early* spring stir the soil lightly.

From 75 to 100 plants will produce all the berries needed for all purposes. Cultivate like corn. As before stated never dig plants from those intended for fruiting. Roots may be taken up in the autumn and cut into pieces about four inches long and packed in sand, keeping them moist but not wet. Buds will soon develop and in the spring plant as are peas or beans. Keep the soil mellow and clean and by the coming fall or spring your plants will be ready for use. And, oh yes! Don't wait till the old patch is worn out before starting a new one. In case the soil crusts around the young plants they must be helped through carefully or they will break and be injured.

There is another species of this fruit known as the Dewberry. The fruit is handsome, pips large, of a deep shining black, juicy, melting and of finest flavor. Its low trailing habit will probably require mulching of straw or other material to prevent the fruit from lying on the ground. In size and quality it equals any of the tall growing sorts. The plants are perfectly hardy, healthy and remarkably productive, with large showy blossoms. The fruit which ripens soon after raspberries is often one and a half inches in length by one inch in diameter. The Dewberry should be found in every garden.

Currants.—This is a fruit found in almost every garden, and of all, we might say, is the most sadly neglected. Hardy, easily cultivated, standing neglect well, but responding liberally to generous treatment, and really no garden is complete without its currant bushes. Its uses are many, but for jelly is quite unsurpassed, while for pies they are also excellent, and when successfully grown for market, either green or ripe, are quite profitable.

They should be set on deep, rich loam and given clean cultivation. The soil cannot be made too rich. As generally found in the garden it is a mass of tangled brush from which the worms have trimmed the leaves, consequently the fruit is small, and few, and far between, whereas if it was judiciously pruned, manured and mulched, the fruit produced would be doubled in size and quantity. Be liberal with manure and you will be liberally rewarded with nice plump rich fruit. In garden culture take good one or two-year-old plants and after having thoroughly prepared the soil by pulverizing, set them 3 by 4 feet apart each way and keep the soil clean and mellow by thorough cultivation and the third year you will reap your reward.

Cultivate shallow to prevent injuring the roots. Prune out the old wood, so that each shoot will have plenty of space in which to grow and so the sun and air may reach all parts of the bush so that the fruit will mature properly. To obtain the best results they should be heavily mulched in the spring, and for this purpose there is nothing better than coal ashes. Straw may also be used. Let no more than five or six shoots grow in each hill. All others should be treated as weeds.

The best way to propagate is by layering. For this purpose use new growth and lay the shoots down in autumn. These may be set out the next spring. Another good way is to make cuttings from new growth; that is, one year old wood. This may be done in early fall as soon as the leaves fall from the bushes. Cut off the ends of the branches about ten inches long; pulverize the soil to the depth of twelve inches; dig holes deep enough to set the cuttings in so that the two top buds will be above ground, then pack the fine soil firmly around the base of the cutting and just at the top of the cutting place the soil more loosely.

Treated in this way they will root before winter and to prevent J. Frost from heaving them out they should be heavily mulched with light manure. This should be carefully drawn away before growth commences in the spring. Or, the cuttings may be made as described and kept in moist sand or buried away from frost and planted in early spring. I prefer the latter way as it gives the plants a start before winter. They must be planted as early as possible. When planted in the fall the soil should be tramped firmly around them in the spring or many of them will die.

The Black varieties have a flavor entirely distinct from the red or white varieties, and, so far as I know are entirely free from the ravages of the Currant worm.

Gooseberry.—Every well kept garden, be it large or small, will contain a generous supply of these, for who is there who does not enjoy Gooseberries in pies, tarts or jam, or when served as fruit when the berries have ripened. This, like other small fruits, is too often sadly neglected, and hence fail and are pronounced "no good," when they are really of very easy culture.

Gooseberries require and delight in a good, rich, loamy soil, with a generous supply of manure each season. They are quite hardy. Regular pruning every season is essential for the production of fine fruit. All varieties, especially English varieties, require a partial shade and should be planted on the north side of a board or picket fence as they are susceptible to the heat of the sun.

They should also be heavily mulched as are blackberries. Mildew often attacks the Gooseberry, to prevent which the bushes should be sprayed as soon as the leaves appear with potassium sulphide (liver of sulphur), one ounce to four gallons of water. This should be done several times during the summer. It is also claimed that cutting out the center of the bushes so as to admit more light and air to penetrate to the fruit will also prevent the berries from mildewing.

They should be set in rows four feet apart and three feet in the row, and do not allow more than six or eight stems to grow in each hill. Cultivate thoroughly and keep free from weeds, and they should be given a dressing of wood ashes annually. Never allow the worms to strip the leaves from the bushes. I think the best time for planting is in the spring as they then become well established before winter.

Gooseberries as well as currants and cane fruits of all kinds commence growth early in the spring, so that where the planting is to be done in the spring it should be done as early as possible. Where fruits of any kind are set out in the autumn they should have a mound of earth placed around them so as to prevent the water standing at their roots; this soil should be tramped firmly around them in the spring. Plant in cool, moist, but not wet soil, as no fruit tree will succeed with wet feet.

Gooseberries are propagated similar to currants, i. e., by laying down branches and covering them with soil. If this is done in the spring they will be ready to set out in the fall and vice versa. New varieties of fruits of all kinds are grown from seed saved from ripe specimens. It is seldom, however, that varieties of special merit are obtained and are therefore often quite valuable.

Coal ashes are a valuable mulch for Gooseberries as well as currants. They keep down the weeds, retain moisture, help to prevent mildew and if sifted on when the foliage is damp will assist in preventing the ravages of the worms. Coal ashes and kitchen slops can be profitably used on small fruits.

Grapes (*Vitis vinifera*).—There is scarcely a yard so small, either in country or town, where room for a few grape vines cannot be found, as they may be admirably trained on the side of a building, on the fences, summer houses, etc., occupying but little room while they supply an abundance of the most healthful fruit; or they may be planted between the rows of berry bushes where these are of sufficient width. The history dates back to the remotest period of which we have any account of the works of man since the deluge of Noah.

Plant in mellow soil which has been deeply plowed. Set the plants a little deeper than they stood in the nursery. Corn or other crops may be planted between the rows the first season. The Grape is among the most wonderful of fruit-bearing plants for longevity, productiveness and the excellence of its fruit. They delight in a high and dry gravelly clay of moderate fertility, with a porous subsoil.

Select well known varieties of first class one or two-year-old vines. With the soil plowed deeply, dig holes wide and deep enough to receive the roots without crowding. Mark out the rows eight feet apart and about the same distance between the vines for the short growing varieties, and for rank growing varieties about twelve feet apart in the row. At the same time plant a large stake in the hole with the vine.

When setting out the vines cut back the plants to two or three eyes, and when growth commences in the spring rub off all but the strongest one and as this grows tie to the stake and pinch off all lateral shoots to one bud. The distance between the vines should vary with the soil; however, a rich soil will require wider planting. It is bad policy to plant too thickly as the fruit will not develop properly.

Before planting, the vines should be properly pruned; the top should be cut back to two or three buds and the roots shortened to about a foot, while the bottom of the holes should be well loosened with the spade or other implement. Some surface soil should be mixed with this dirt before the vine is set. Keep the roots moist while planting. The roots should be well spread in the hole and covered with surface soil pressed firmly around them; then fill the hole with mellow soil. This also holds good when planting any kind of plant.

Never use strong manure next the roots; if used, place it on the surface. Compost is good to mix with the soil. Bone dust or ashes are the best of fertilizers where the soil needs enriching. As the future growth, health and productiveness of the Grape depend very much on its getting a good "start" in the world, good culture as for any other crop should be generously given. During summer keep the vines well cultivated, allowing no weeds or grass to grow. The surface soil especially should be frequently stirred.

In the fall cut the vines back to two or three buds and in the spring before growth commences rub off all but two and tie the vines to the stakes. Then in the fall cut these two canes back to three or four feet, according to the strength of the vines. Young vines will sometimes bear a few bunches the second year, but it is best not to let them bear until the third season.

At the beginning of the third year the trellis should be set up. Posts are set up between two vines and to these wires or slats are fastened. Wires are best as the wind has less effect on them and the vines cling to them. These wires are placed one above the other, the lowest one about two feet from the ground. The canes are bent horizontaly and fastened to the lower wire and four or five buds allowed to grow, and each bud will set two or three more bunches. The fourth season two of the canes on each arm are permitted to grow, while the others are pruned to one bud, and from these the canes for next year's fruiting are allowed to grow.

The fruiting canes must be cut back when they grow three leaves beyond the top clusters on the cane. It must be borne in mind that no fruit comes from old wood, but only from that of previous season's growth. The soil should be cultivated thoroughly in the early part of the season.

Where pruning is done in the autumn the vines should be taken from the trellis and laid on the ground and if they do not stay down, some dirt should be thrown on the ends of the canes to hold them. It is not always necessary to do this, but is a precaution against winter killing. In regard to the time in which to trim there is difference of opinion, but I prefer the month of February, as our most severe winter is over and the sap has not commenced to flow to any great extent and will not before the wounds have healed so as to prevent bleeding.

It has been well and truthfully said that "small fruits in the country are like Heaven—objects of universal desire and general neglect." There are various modes of trimming the Grape in this and other countries; "The short spur system," "The long cane system," "The close cut system," and "The horizontal arm system." The latter I prefer, as I believe it to be more in accordance with nature and it has many advantages over the other modes, although each have proven a success in various locations.

The close cut system consists in cutting all the wood of the previous year's growth back to the main stalk, depending solely on the latent buds for the next crop. The short spur system consists in cutting the canes back to one bud of the main vine. The long cane system consists in pruning out the two-year wood that bore fruit the year previous and cutting the new canes back to the length of two or three feet as circumstances permit. This mode is in universal use. The horizontal arm system consists in a main vine extending each way from the stalk on the lower wire and the growth of the year previous cut back to two or three buds of the main arm or vine. Where the thinning process is in vogue, which consists in cutting out the surplus shoots before they blossom, the summer pruning is done by destroying all surplus shoots that start during the summer.

When pruning always employ the same system as was used the previous season. Use manure as a mulch and do not place it directly on the roots. Do not allow the vines to be overgrown by weeds or you will get very little reward from your vine. Soil and situation make a great deal of difference in flavor. Those grown on gravelly soil will be the richest and sweetest.

Although our space is quite limited we realize that a treatise on the subject we have chosen for our book would not be quite complete without a few words on the above subject. While we cannot treat the subject at any great length we will endeavor to give a few "helps" in the destruction of these pests.

Cabbage Flea (*Haltica striolata*).—This is the first insect of any importance that appears, and is the little black flea that attacks the cabbage, cauliflower, turnip, radish, etc., and in fact all plants belonging to the natural order *Cruciferæ*. Not only does the flea destroy the first leaves, but the larvae feed upon the roots of the plants.

Soot, ashes, lime (slacked), and dust scattered on the leaves is an effectual remedy. This must be done while the plants are wet and after every rain. Soap suds applied to the roots will destroy the larvae.

Cabbage Worm.—The cabbage worm, the larvae of the common white butterfly (*Pieris rapae*), may be destroyed in several ways. That of hand picking is effectual but tedious and not to be desired.

Kerosene emulsion, ashes, hellebore, saltpetre water, bran and road dust. Pyrethrum powder dusted into the heads is sure death to every worm. It should be mixed with five times its bulk of plaster. The application of liquid insecticides will not prove very satisfactory on account of the peculiar structure of the leaves which allows the water to roll off in drops and does not adhere to any part of them. Washing the heads out with cold water every day or two while the sun is shining hotly will destroy the eggs. The vessel containing the water should be held above the plants allowing the water to fall from a height, or it may

be applied with a force pump.   Poisonous substances are
unsafe and not to be recommended.

Cut Worms (*Agrostes, Leucania, Mamestra, Hadena, Nephelodes*).—Of this pest there are several species including the Army Worm (*Leucania unipuncta*). They do their work during the night and may be destroyed with parisgreen or a piece of sod may be inverted by each plant; the worms will gather under these and they may then be caught and killed.

Striped Cucumber Bug (*Diabrotica vittata*).—This pest which makes itself quite numerous may be kept in check by the use of plaster, tobacco scattered close to the hill, by poisons, or by cultivating every day or two. Another method is to take a bottomless box twelve inches square and six or eight inches deep and cover it with mosquito netting. One of these inverted over each hill until the plants are in rough leaf will be a sure protection.

Squash Bug (*Anasa tristis*.—This is the common "stink" bug and will, if not destroyed, soon destroy the vines. They come in pairs and if the first are killed before the eggs are deposited there will be but little trouble, but if not destroyed they will raise large families and become quite numerous. They may be destroyed by the application of kerosene emulsion. The eggs should be gathered at least bi-weekly and all rubbish burned early in the fall.

Squash Borer (*Melittia ceto*).—This pest destroys the vines by boring into the roots and destroying the pith. Late planting of main crop; destroying the vines attacked as soon as crop is harvested; and destroying moths.

Asparagus Beetle (*Crioceris asparagi*).—Prompt actions, dusting with lime, arsenical mixtures of paris green and london purple. See also asparagus culture.

Onion Maggot.—The larvae of the onion fly (*Anthomyia ceparum*). The eggs are laid in May or June, on the leaves near the ground. The maggots burrow into the bulb, causing them to decay. Dig and burn the affected onions, but for the best mode of destruction see onion culture.

Celery Fly (*Anthomyia ceparum*).—Dusting the plants with soot or lime will prevent the fly from laying its eggs; but the most effectual way is to crush the leaves when the larvae (grub) is discovered.

Mealy Bug.—Fumigating with tobacco will effectually destroy them.

Red Spider.—Frequent syringing will keep down the attacks of this pest.

Green Lice (*Aphides*).—Use kerosene emulsion.

Snails.—Soot, salt or lime are a sure remedy when scattered on the ground.

Ants.—Destroy their nests and sprinkle sulphur where they frequent.

Wire Worms (*Drasterius elegans, Melanotus fissilis, etc*).—There are about a dozen species of this pest. Place a small potato under the surface of the soil; this makes an excellent trap. This may be poisoned. Fall plowing and rotation of crops is also recommended.

Currant Worm (*Nematus ventricosus*).—The currant worm should be destroyed promptly with insect powder or hellebore, the latter—one ounce to two gallons of water. Or better still, throw wood ashes through the bushes while wet. There are many methods recommended but the above is quite effectual, is easily and cheaply applied and is perfectly harmless. Apply after every rain and as soon as the worms appear.

Potato Beetle (*Doryphora 10-lineata*).—This is the common Colorado potato bug and has evidently come to stay. Paris green applied in the form of a spray or dusted on the foliage is the most easily applied and cheap remedy, but care must be exercised in its use wherever used that none may get where animals, etc., are liable to get at it.

Bean Weevil (*Bruchus oblectus*) and **Pea Weevil** (*Bruchus pisorum*).—Place the seed to be treated in air tight boxes, place some bisulphide of carbon (very inflamable) in open vessels and place on top of seed. Cover to exclude the air and let it remain for twenty-four hours.

Strawberry Weevil (*Anthononeus signatus*).—Spraying with paris green.

Strawberry Crownborer (*Tyloderma fragariae*).—The eggs are laid on the crowns in June or July and when hatched the grub burrows into and destroys the plants. The worm is white, about one-fifth of an inch long, and has a yellow head. Burn all infected plants, or plow up the bed.

Grapeberry Moth (*Eudemis botrana*).—The larvae eats the pulp and part of the seed; is quite destructive. No good remedy known.

In fighting Injurious Insects it is always best to avoid the use of poisonous substances wherever possible to do so, especially if there are children about, for they are liable to get at the berries on which the poisons have been used, and, too, it is not safe to use berries, cabbage, cauliflower, melons, etc., that have been poisoned as some of the substance is liable to remain on them and cause serious results.

KEROSENE EMULSION (*Insecticide*), How to make.—Take one-quarter pound of hard soap, cut up and dissolve in two quarts of boiling rain water; while hot stir in one pint of kerosene. Stir briskly until no oil rises on the top. Add water to make two gallons. While not in the least bit dangerous, this is sure death to all kinds of plant lice. Apply in the form of a spray or with the sprinkler.

BORDEAUX MIXTURE (*Fungicide*), To make.—Dissolve six pounds of sulphate of copper (copperas, green vitrol) in a tub or earthen vessel (metal vessels should not be used), and in another vessel slake four pounds of fresh lime, adding water sufficient to reduce it to the consistency of thick lime wash. This should be slowly poured into the copper solution straining it through a coarse cloth. An old fertilizer (gunny) sack is excellent for this purpose. To this mixture add sufficient water to make about fifty gallons.

When desired a combined insecticide and fungicide may be made by adding one-quarter pound of paris green to the mixture. Apply in the form of a spray. It is quite poisonous. In using care must be exercised that none of the mixture falls on the grass where stock or poultry can get it. It is also well to remember that all liquid poisons should be kept well stirred while applying them, so that the poisonous substances will be thoroughly mixed and evenly distributed. Some spray pumps do this automatically and are preferable.

How to Make and Manage the Lawn.

In preparing the Lawn see that the work is well and properly executed, and if needed have the soil thoroughly drained, as wet soil will not do for this purpose. Where the work is properly done it will last for years, while if done in a slip-shod fashion it will be a continual source of annoyance. Where there are any old stumps or rocks in the plot they should be dug out and the holes filled with soil. This should be packed firmly to prevent its settling and making holes. The surface should be perfectly even and smooth for various reasons. All hollows should have the sod taken from them and the holes filled with loam from elsewhere. Also remove all bumps from the surface.

Now go over the Lawn and destroy every weed you may find in it. If you cannot pull them, pry them up with a digging fork, then pull them out and press the soil firmly. The soil should be harrowed and raked to reduce it to as fine a condition as possible as well as to level it, as nothing detracts from the appearance of a Lawn more than an uneven surface. Now your ground is ready and next that concerns you is the seed.

Just as early as the weather is open and the soil free from frost and dry enough to work the seed should be sown. If one harrowing isn't enough harrow it again. Now take wooden rakes and rake off all the rubbish that may be there and remove it as you go along. After this if your soil is as good and rich as it should be on the surface it will now be ready for the seed; but if the soil is poor, recuperate it by giving a good dressing of compost composed of one-third or one-half of loam and the other half or two-thirds of well rotted manure. Spread this on to a thickness of one or two inches. This should be done immediately. Bone meal is also an excellent fertilizer for the Lawn as it is lasting in its effects and is also free from noxious seeds. About 600 to 1000 pounds should be used per acre. The time to sow the seed will vary with circumstances, but late in March or early in April is a good time. It will not be necessary to roll the soil, as the snows and rains will have compacted it sufficiently.

The top dressing won't hurt the grass there may be at this time, but on the contrary will be a benefit to it, causing it to come up with renewed vigor, but it will not be even or thick enough and will require fresh seed sown all over it to get it equally green and in even sod. When sowing time comes break the crust that may have formed on the soil. For this a brush harrow is excellent; after this rake off the litter and cart it away. Then sow the seed broadcast and rake lightly and roll the soil firmly so as to cover the seed about a quarter of an inch deep. The seed should be of the best obtainable and should be a mixture of the finest varieties, embracing such as are hardy and of neat growth and best adapted to produce a permanent and fine turf throughout the season.

As different varieties of grasses mature at different seasons, some early, others late, a mixture is absolutely necessary to produce a continual bright green. The following mixture is a good one: Two bushels Kentucky blue grass, two bushels red top, one bushel rye grass, six pounds of white clover; mix and sow at the rate of two to four bushels, according to circumstances. The rye grass is for quick growth and must not be sown thick enough to injure the two finer grasses. Though disliked by some, clover is excellent on clayey or stiff soil. The seed should be mixed with finely sifted loam or should be sown on a quiet day. Keep the seed well mixed or the clover will fall to the bottom of the heap. This may be prevented by mixing the seed with loam or sand as above.

As stated above no one kind of grass will answer as it will not keep beautifully green all through the season but a mixture of several is necessary, as some are more luxuriant in early spring, others in summer and again others in autumn, and a proper combination of these various varieties is necessary to make a neat, velvety lawn. Old Lawns will be greatly benefitted if they are carefully raked so as to remove the leaves and dead grass that may be on them and then sprinkled with the above mixture which will renew the thin spots and places that have been killed by the winter or other causes. Then give it a thorough rolling with a heavy roller. When building a new lawn and after it is graded the first thing is to give the entire surface a thick dressing of black loam. This should be done in all cases wherever possible. The Lawn must have a good foundation to be beautiful as it should be. Where the ground is sloping it will require a heavier dressing than where it is level, as heavy rains may wash the top soil away, especially before the grass has become thoroughly established.

The surface should be level and smooth as possible. One-half the seed should be sown in one direction and the other at right angles. Water should be used freely on Lawns as this gives that healthy appearance so greatly admired. No matter how much seed of a certain variety you may sow on a certain space it will support only so many plants, while if another variety is sown in connection with it a largely increased number of plants will be obtained as they thrive on different elements of the soil.

Lawns must be kept rich if you desire a good, fresh, green, velvety crop of grass. As Lawn grass is a voracious feeder it will not thrive and hold its color unless it receives sufficient nourishment. The reason there are so many rusty, dingy Lawns is because this point is too little appreciated. A well fed Lawn is always a velvety one and is sure to be admired.

Mowing repeatedly year after year and raking off the leaves that fall from the trees, which neatness makes necessary, and which removes a valuable top dressing annually, requires artificial top dressing yearly of short, thoroughly decayed manure, or a dressing of commercial fertilizer in the amounts given. Stable manure is in some respects unpleasant to handle, ill looking and quite odorous, and if used should be applied late in the autumn. Where done earlier it defaces the Lawn at a season when it proves offensive. Fine dry manure which is easily pulverized is best as it spreads neatly and evenly over the surface. This is quite essential or one spot will be over-nourished while another will be starved. But if this cannot be had coarse manure may be used if *spread* evenly as possible, while if there happens to be a sharp November freeze followed by a thaw it will loosen the lumps and cause them to pulverize quite easily. This may be done with a smoothing harrow which will also spread them over the surface in a most commendable manner.

Always prepare your soil thoroughly and sow the seed thickly in order to obtain a good growth at once, and press the soil firmly. Second only to that necessity—good seed—is time of sowing, quantity to use (be sure to use plenty), preparation, etc. It was at one time considered that the clippings should be left on the lawn to act as a mulch, thus returning to the soil what it had extracted during growth. This, however, soon proved a mistake, as the dried grass, besides looking unsightly, prevented roots from tillering out and instead of its improving would soon ruin any Lawn if left on. The best way is as soon as the mowing is done to carefully rake up all the clippings and depend upon manuring in the winter to keep up the growth sufficiently to make a thick, velvety growth of verdure.

As before stated there is nothing more essential in the adornment of the home than a neat, close-cut, well-kept lawn with a velvety turf dotted here and there with beds of flowers, for without it the palace would look dingy and the finest flowering plants and bedding scenes are insignificant, while with it the most lowly cottage makes us feel that there is really "no place like home."

Where they are to be had, rocks or various shaped stones may be utilized to make borders for the flower beds, etc., as they may be placed in various forms and when whitewashed or painted make a pleasing contrast with the foliage of the plants. They may also be built up to a height of a foot or more in any desired form and the inside filled with soil in which plants may be planted with pleasing effect. Shells of various shapes may also be used for borders or the edges of walks, etc.

Every Lawn should have nicely graveled walks laid out and the edges kept nicely trimmed. Where there are curves in these walks let them be graceful and not too abrupt or they will detract from the general appearance of the Lawn. To make the surroundings still more attractive the Lawn should be appropriately planted with trees and shrubs. On the smaller yards the largest growing trees are not desirable, or, if planted, it should be with a view of removing them when they become too large, and thus injure by their shade the other occupants of the soil.

As a guide it may be well to say that in the arrangement of the trees and shrubs they should be set irregularly along the sides of the lawn and bordering to some extent the front. Only such varieties should be used as are conspicuous for their beauty of form or foliage, or both, and the flowering shrubs should be selected with reference to their continual blooming from spring to autumn.

In front of the main rooms of the dwelling and next the graveled walks can be beds of fancy foliaged plants such as begonias, coleus, dracenas, etc., and bright blooming flowers such as geraniums, petunias, cockscombs and phlox, while somewhat more expensive are the carpet beds or mosaic bed set with plants of high colored foliage. These beds, if well cared for, will make a pleasing sight throughout the summer until destroyed by frost. These are popular because they produce the effect desired—looking their very prettiest during the fine season of the year. They cannot be depended on for blooming, for they are not for that purpose; and a provision for a supply of flowers should be made for that purpose elsewhere.

The beds should be of various forms; stars, crescents, circles, ovals, Maltese crosses, etc. These may be considered as examples from which one can deviate in numberless ways in the forms and sizes of beds and the plants used in filling them, but always subserving the laws of good taste and color blending, and if you have an eye for the beautiful you will be well paid for all trouble in endeavoring to make home beautiful by its surrounding attractions.

Notes on Their Culture.

"Flowers are God's Jewels for earth's adornment."

Nothing adds more to the appearance of the home than its surroundings. After giving instructions on the building of the lawn, the next point which comes under our consideration is the cultivation of Flora's treasures—Flowers. The pleasure to be derived from the cultivation of Flowers is known only in its fullest extent to those who have watched every day's mysterious developments from the sowing of the tiny seed to the grand display of the fully developed plant.

In spite of good seed and careful management, there must come now and again unaccountable failure and disappointment. Experienced growers sometimes fail, and try again with the same seed and succeed, so do not be discouraged by an occasional failure, for you will have to contend with unfavorable weather, insects, and numerous adverse circumstances; but these are but the background of the picture—the little trials which make the eventual success so sweet.

In raising Flowers from seed, not only care but knowledge is required—knowledge of the requirements of the different classes of Flowers—annuals, biennials, perrenials and the tender greenhouse Flowers. A careful perusal of the following notes, though brief, will be of advantage to the inexperienced.

Flower seeds may be sown in the open ground as soon as the soil becomes dry and easily crumbled after spring frosts have disappeared. They may be sown in the borders where they are intended to bloom, or in seed pans or beds and transplanted to their flowering beds. The latter is the best plan, especially with very small seeds such as pansy, as it enables the plants to become established earlier, and also because during the period of early growth the soil occupied is not attractive. There must be discretion exercised as to the depth to which seeds should be covered—

small delicate seeds merely on the surface, some barely pressed into the soil, and others fully one-quarter inch deep —the depth in every instance being regulated by the size of the seed itself. As the sprouts of small seeds must necessarily be small, if sown as deep as large seed they will be unusually late in starting or more likely will perish in the ground after germinating, for want of strength to break through the surface.

Seedling plants can be nearly as well grown in the window of a sitting room or parlor—provided the temperature is right—as in a greenhouse, for seeds do not require a direct light while germinating. The best things to sow seeds in are pans or boxes (tobacco boxes are nice, as the smell of the tobacco drives away insects to a large degree) two or three inches deep with crack in the bottoms through which the water can drain quickly, which is quite essential. The soil should be of equal parts of good garden loam and sand thoroughly mixed and passed through a sieve. Fill the boxes to within half an inch of the rim, and press the soil as firm and level as possible. Now sow the seed, scattering it evenly over the surface. With a common sieve dust just as much soil over the seed as will cover it. Then dampen the soil carefully with a spray or otherwise, being careful not to "wash" the soil.

If the box is kept at a temperature of about 60°, giving it a shower of spray whenever the soil appears dry, very few seeds will fail to germinate. The average period of germination of seeds is from ten to fourteen days, but some seeds of a hard body often lie dormant for weeks or even months. The Acacia, Clematis, Polyanthus and others are examples of this.

Germination of such seeds will be greatly accelerated by placing them in a cup of lukewarm water allowing them to soak for a few hours before sowing. And in many Flowers the period of blooming will be extended by picking off the blooms when past their best, thus preventing the strength of the plants being exhausted in the ripening of the seed pods.

As soon as the seedlings appear they will require careful attention, and should have as much sun and air as possible on pleasant days. Prick out of the seed pans or boxes into other pans or boxes, placing them about one inch apart, and shading from the sun for a few days until they are well established. When large enough they may be planted separately in pots, and kept till the proper season arrives for planting in the open—that is when there is no danger of frost.

Some varieties of hardy Flowers such as Sweet Peas, Convolvulus, etc., are best sown where they are to grow, but none but the most hardy varieties of Flowers should be sown in the open ground until both soil and air have become warm—about corn planting time. It is a good plan to sow only a part of your seed at first, and then in a week or so the remainder. The thinning out of plants in their earlier stages is quite important.

It is always best to sow thicker than the plants are required for various reasons, but if the young plants are allowed to remain in a crowded condition they soon spoil each other; they must therefore be thinned out, but with caution. At first remove only enough to give the remainder clear space in which to grow, and more when they are two or three inches high. The number of plants left at the final thinning must depend on the size and habits of the plants themselves—if large and spreading single plants are to be preferred, if not of a spreading nature two or three may remain, at equal distances apart. In all cases begin thinning in time, before they become crowded.

Plants may be transplanted whenever large enough to handle. Lift them carefully with the aid of a trowel, retaining as much of the soil as will adhere to the roots. Moisten the soil in the boxes before disturbing the plants. Transplanting should be done in wet or cloudy weather. If the soil is dry a good soaking with water before and after transplanting is advisable. Shade from the sun for a few days.

The importance of uniform attention to watering will soon be learned by observation and experience, but the inexperienced cultivator may be reminded that to allow the young germs to get parched, as well as too frequent and irregular watering, often leads to the loss of the whole. Plants in pots should only be watered when the surface of the soil becomes dry—not daily or at stated times, as is too often practiced, but when necessity requires it.

Liquid manure is quite beneficial to plants whose roots are confined in pots, but should never be given to very young plants, or oftener than twice a week and always in small quantities. It is advisable to smoke pot plants every few days with tobacco smoke to prevent the ravages of the green fly. The cause will usually be found in the plant being root bound, to avoid which re-pot frequently during the growing season. Heat and moisture are quite essential to the germination of all seeds but as these cannot be regulated in the open ground, seeds of tender plants require the assistance of the hotbed or cold frame.

In making a selection of Flowers, everyone should have the beautiful annuals and perennials. A small collection will furnish an abundance for the entire summer—the Aster, Antirrhinum, Balsam, Dianthus, Delphinium, Pansy, Petunia, Phlox, Portulaca, Stocks, Verbena and Double Zinnia, should have a place in your collection. For a low edge there is nothing better than the Sweet Pea and Nasturtium; while for fragrance there must be Mignonette, Sweet Alyssum, Pinks and Carnations. For masses of color and ribbon border there is a wide field to choose from—the Phlox in its many distinct colors is one of the best for this purpose. Candytuft is neat and makes nice button hole bouquets, while a few Everlastings and Ornamental Grasses will come in nicely for indoor decoration in the winter. Then the beautiful Gladioli among the tall summer Flowers; the Dahlia for autumn, while the Lily is unsurpassed in its graceful beauty.

Flowers raised from seed are known as Annuals, Biennials and Perennials.

ANNUALS.—For the best summer display the garden is dependent on this class which is grown from seed sown every spring, as they arrive at maturity, bloom, produce seeds and die in one season. They are sub-divided in three classes, hardy, half-hardy and tender. Hardy Annuals are those which require no artificial heat at any period of their growth. Every stage of their growth from the germination to the ripening of the seed may be passed in the open ground. They are the most easily cultivated of all plants. As a rule Annuals may be sown in the open ground about corn-planting time or when the weather has become settled. For a succession sow at intervals from March to September. Seeds of the hardier Annuals may be sown where they are to flower; but as a rule it is preferable to transplant, as the plants are generally stronger and stand drought better. During very warm, dry weather and when the seedlings are first set out they should be watered frequently. If the weeds are kept in check as they should be and the soil frequently stirred the plants will receive the full benefit of the rains and dews, which they will not if the soil is allowed to become hard and weedy. Half-hardy Annuals are those species that require artificial heat in the earlier stages of their growth but bloom and ripen their seeds in the open air. They should be sown in pans or boxes in a gentle heat in February or March. By the end of March or early in April they will be ready for transplanting to their beds in the open, but previous to this they should be hardened by gradual exposure night and day.

BIENNIALS as a rule do not flower until the second season from the sowing of the seed, and are only at their best one season, and for a limited time only. They are not therefore adapted for a bed on the lawn, which should make a show of blooms all through the season.

PERENNIALS.—This class is composed of herbaceous plants, which die down during winter, but spring up at the return of spring and produce new stems annually. Many of the species improve by age, forming large clumps or bushes; by being divided, the stock is increased and the plant invigorated. Some of this class of plants like Antirrhinum, Dianthus, Pansy, Stock, etc., flower the first season, but true Perennials, like Biennials, do not flower until the second season.

Hardy Biennials and Perennials require the same treatment as hardy Annuals. If seeds of these three classes are sown in boxes in March or April and so sheltered in a good cold frame they will make strong plants by spring and will bloom earlier, in the case of Biennials and Perennials a season earlier. Or they may be planted in the open soil in March and on the approach of winter mulched with leaves, evergreen boughs, straw or litter as a protection against frost. In spring this covering must be carefully removed and the soil around them loosened, and when large enough transplant them to where they are to remain.

Tender ANNUALS, BIENNIALS and PERENNIALS for window and greenhouse culture.—The best method to obtain an early bloom and to insure strength and vigor to the plants is to sow the seeds in pans early, placing them in a warm partially shaded window or warm greenhouse, or plunging in a moderate hotbed, carefully protecting them from the cold, shading from the midday sun and watering with a fine spray. The seeds require extra care in sowing, as they are very small and delicate. The pans or boxes must be thoroughly drained and should have a layer of stones or broken pots in the bottom. The seed should be sown in a very light rich compost, composed of two-thirds rich loam, one-third sand and thoroughly decayed cow manure, thoroughly mixed together. Make the surface smooth by pressing it with a board, and sprinkle a little sand over it; water with a fine spray. After the pans have drained, the seed should be evenly and carefully sown. Cover them very little, if at all. After sowing place the pans in a close frame, kept shaded as exposure for only a short time to the rays of the sun is enough to scorch the extremely delicate leaves and tiny roots of the plants. Water frequently, particularly if the house or frame is very warm.

Directly the plants are large enough to handle—2 or 3 inches high—they must be transplanted into other pans prepared as for seed sowing, and allowed to grow until they touch each other; then shift into small pots and place in the cold frame. When the roots fill these pots, shift again in larger pots. They will not thrive if replaced in frame or placed on shelves in greenhouse near the glass. Re-pot as required. If troubled with the green fly fumigate with tobacco. The varieties belonging to this class are the Abutilon, Begonias, Chrysanthemums, Coleus, Cyclamen, Ferns, Gloxinias, etc. They may be planted in the lawn when they have attained sufficient size; this however should not be done before the end of May.

Latin Terms.

The meaning of some of the most frequently used Latin terms in the names of Flowers: Album or alba, *white*, argenta, *silver*; atropurpurea, *dark purple*; aurea, *yellow;* bicolor, *two colored*; tri-color, *of three colors;* striata, *striped;* candidissima, *pure white;* coccinea, *scarlet;* coerulea, *blue;* flammula, *flame color;* lutea, *yellow;* marmorata, *marbled*; multicolor, *of many colors*; punctata, *spotted*; purpurea, *purple*; roseum, *rose* or *red*; rubra, *dark red*; sanguineous, *blood red;* compacta, *compact*; densiflorus, *close flowered*; elegans, *graceful*; fragrans, *sweet scented*; flore pleno, *double flowered*; semi pleno, *half double*; grandiflora, *large flowered*; major, *tall*; minor, *small*, *dwarf*; maximum, *tallest*; monstrosum, *monstrous*; nanus, *dwarf*; odorata, *sweet scented*; pyramidalis, *pyramidal shaped*; robusta, *strong*.

Abbreviations: Ha, hardy annual; hha, half-hardy annual; ta, tender annual; hb, hardy biennial; hhb, half-hardy biennial; hp, hardy perennial; hhp, half-hardy perennial; gp, greenhouse perennial; gc, greenhouse climber; gs, greenhouse shrubs.

Calendar of Garden Operations for the Year.

In a country so vast and varied as is ours, where the setting of the sun in the east is the rising of the sun in the west, and the summer of the south is the winter of the north, and the influences of soil and climate so widely differ, it is impossible to give a calendar of operations to suit all sections at the same time of the year. From this reason the tiller of the soil must be guided by his own location, soil and climatic influences.

January.—This is one of the winter months of this section, when there is little or nothing to be done with the soil. In favorable weather prepare hotbeds and cold frames for the future use of cabbage, egg plants and other plants that are to be grown for transplanting, Dress asparagus beds, trim fruit and shade trees and spread thoroughly decayed manure on lawns; mix with it some lawn grass seed. See that all unoccupied land has been thoroughly plowed and left in ridges to derive as much benefit as possible from the action of the frost, which tends to lighten and sweeten the soil. Burn rubbish and scatter the ashes over the roots of fruit trees. See that celery in trenches and vegetables in pits are *thoroughly* protected. Attend to plants in frames and protect from insect pests. Force hyacinths and all bulb flower roots. Along the Gulf plant Irish potatoes, peas, lettuce, radishes, etc.

February.—Get ready for early planting. In milder sections, if the weather permits, transplant trees, berry bushes, rose bushes and horseradish. Get in manure; let it be well incorporated before sowing; fresh manure applied directly to your crop may ruin it. If any pruning of small fruits has been neglected see to it now. Towards end of month sow tomatoes, peppers, cauliflowers, egg plants, etc. Sow perennials for early blooming. Mulch trees, bushes and vines. Dress lawns. Plant the following for early use if the climate and weather are favorable: Beans, beets, carrots, parsnips, spinach, radishes, lettuce, potatoes and other hardy varieties. Mulch rhubarb and asparagus. Turn all soil not turned previously. Transplant a few hardy plants to be nursed for extra early use.

March.—Prepare the soil for seeding when in proper condition. Replant where seeds have failed to grow. Sow seeds as in February. Thin plants where needed. Salt asparagus beds. Plant sweet corn. Pull the weeds. In northern states start your hotbeds and trim and mulch. Horseradish may be set in any spare corner. Spread manure everywhere.

April.—A busy month as far north as Ohio in the family garden, but don't plant until soil and weather are favorable. Hardy varieties may be sown in favored spots. Plant as in last month with the addition of more tender plants at the end of the month. Replant where seeds have failed. Stir the soil around plants and kill weeds. Farther north trim shrubs of all kinds and care for lawns. Use the lawn mower and scatter seeds on bare spots. Keep all soil occupied.

May.—High culture. All seeds may be sown this month as far north as Ohio. Stir the soil frequently around plants, but don't disturb the roots. Brush early peas and sow later ones. Thin plants in beds and transplant tomatoes, etc., as soon as large enough to handle. Prepare ground for celery. Sow cabbage, cauliflowers, etc., for late use. Fight weeds and insects. Sow flower seeds. Plant lima beans.

June.—Everything is doing nicely and in full growth. The hoe should have daily exercise. Transplant celery, tomatoes, sweet potatoes, late cabbage, kill weeds, and prepare soil for turnips. Use ground that has matured early crops. Keep the soil mellow to retain moisture and destroy weeds. Hill potatoes and water transplanted plants daily in the evening. Clear ground for succession and plant second crop. Sow perennials and biennials now. Dress asparagus beds with salt. Replant corn.

July.—To induce quick growth cultivate often and give liquid manure. Where the ground is clear dress with manure, spade deeply and plant Brussels sprouts, kale, broccoli, cabbage, etc. Destroy weeds before the seeds mature. Sow more turnips and snap beans for succession. Kill insects. Nip the tips from runner beans. Trim tomato plants and tie a few to stakes if you want ripe fruit early and lucious. Look for bugs on vine crops. Mulch strawberry beds with old manure after rains.

August.—Plants set out last month should now be strong. Southern gardens should be planted for a second crop of vegetables such as beans, beets, carrots, cabbage, potatoes and tomatoes. Cut out old brush from berry bushes to encourage new growth. Destroy weeds on vacant ground. Strawberries set out this month will bear next season. Cut out wild grass and weeds from the lawn. Early cabbage sown now will keep for winter. Earth up celery. Dig potatoes when ripe. Hardy flowers may now be sown. Early beans may give a crop of snaps if sown early in the month. Pot calceolarias.

September.—Turnips, mustard and parsley may now be sown. Celery fully grown should be well banked and watered and the tops protected from the sun. Gather matured crops. In the south sow peas, onions and radishes for winter use. Set out berry bushes and trees and mulch to prevent the frost from heaving them out. Look out for frost. Pot bulbs for early bloom.

October.—Pull the weeds in turnip beds; if green throw them on the compost heap, if ripe burn them. Sow seed on the lawn. Look after your compost heaps and don't let the rains injure them. Add to them as much as possible and turn over during frosty weather. Mulch berry bushes with manure, and cover the strawberry beds between the rows with leaves or litter. Trim fruit and shade trees. Select seeds and store carefully. Make general clearance of remains of gathered crops and fallen leaves and put them in the compost heap. They are very valuable. Set out trees and mulch them. Dig all vacant land. Tomato vines may be pulled and hung in a warm place to mature the green specimens. Plant hyacinths, tulips, narcissus, etc., for spring flowering. Prepare for winter.

November.—A continuation of the general work of last month. Plow or spade your garden and scatter manure everywhere and leave to the actions of the frost. Prune trees and vines and burn the brush to destroy insects. Transplant fruit trees of all kinds and mulch. Dress your lawn with fine manure. Gather late crops and store for winter. Put your frames away for winter. Give celery in trenches extra protection. Mulch strawberry beds to prevent heaving. Lay cuttings to increase your supply of small fruit plants.

December.—In the southern states sow radishes, onions, peas and potatoes. Prepare hotbeds and sow cabbage, tomatoes, etc., for early planting. Prune trees, vines, rosebushes and shrubs. Cover lawns with manure and re-seed where needed. Plow every part of the garden that has not been so treated and cover with manure. Fork over your compost heaps to promote decay, keeping them flat on top. Cover with boards to protect from storms and subsequent loss. Procure leaf mold and store for future use. See that your garden is well drained before planting time. Burn rubbish and scatter ashes over roots of trees. Repetition in these hints is for different latitudes.

Wishing you a prosperous New Year.

Conclusion.

And now, kind reader, having borne me company through these pages our task is accomplished; we have come to the end of our little book, and must here part company. It is my hope you have received some benefit from the hints I have given, for my endeavor has been to make them plain and practical throughout and easily understood by even the most inexperienced.

To those who have never been interested in the "Garden and its Management" we will once more that you miss a great many excellent and … your table throughout the year—dishes both wholesome, healthful and appetizing; while if you are interested in your work as you should be much pleasure and knowledge as well as profit will be derived from the culture of plants both "Vegetable" and "Flowering."

And now, may you be favored with your share of rain and sunshine for without these our efforts would be in vain, as they are necessary for the well doing of all life—plant as well as animal. Remember, too, that "that which is worth doing at all is worth doing well." This applies to nothing more forcibly than in the management of the garden.

Before parting company I trust we have been of mutual benefit one to the other and that you will take a more kindly interest in the Garden and its Management than heretofore, if this is possible. So wishing you much success in your labors, I beg to remain

Your faithful, sincere and humble servant,

JNO. T. TEAT,

Feb. 12th, '98.   Cardington, O.

INDEX.

The Farmer's Garden and Its Management.

	PAGE
Author's Preface	3
Introductory	5-24
The Location	7-8
The Soil of the Garden	9
Preparing the Soil	9-10
Tools	10-13
Laying out the Garden	13-14
Compost	14
Manure	14-16
Fertilizers	16
Procuring Supplies, Seeds, Plants, Etc.	16-17
Raising Plants	17-19
Watering and Transplanting	19-20
Saving Seed	20
Hot-beds—Illustrated	21-23
Cold Frame	23-24

Cultural Notes—What to Grow and How to Grow It—Illustrated.

Artichokes	25-26
Asparagus	26-28
Beans	28-30
Beets	31
Borecole or Kale	32
Broccoli	32-33
Brussels Sprouts	33
Cabbage	33-36
Carrots	36-37
Cauliflower	37-38
Celery	38-40
Chives	40
Chicory	41
Collards	41-42
Corn Salad	42
Corn, Sugar	42-43
Corn, Pop	43-44
Cress	44-45
Cucumber	45-46
Dandelion	47
Endive	47-48
Egg Plant	48
Garlic	49
Horseradish	49
Herbs, Culture and Manner of Using	49-51
Kohl-Rabi	51-52
Leek	52

	PAGE
Lettuce	52-53
Melon, Musk	53-54
Melon, Water	54-55
Mustard	55
Mushrooms	55-56
Okra	56-57
Onion	57-59
Parsley	59-60
Parsnip	60
Peas	60-61
Peanut	61-62
Peppers	62-63
Pumpkin	63
Potatoes, Sweet	63-64
Potatoes, Irish	64-67
Radish	67
Rhubarb or Pie-Plant	67-69
Sage	69
Salsify	69-70
Spinach	70
Squash	70-71
Turnip	71-73
Storing Vegetables for Winter Use	72
Tomato	73-74
Quantity of Seed Required to Produce a given Number of Plants and to Sow an Acre of Ground	75-76
Number of Trees, Plants or Shrubs	77-78

Small Fruits—Illustrated.

Strawberry	79-81
Raspberry	81-82
Blackberry	82-84
Currants	84-85
Gooseberry	85-86
Grapes	86-88
Injurious Insects	89-92
Kerosene Emulsion	92
Bordeaux Mixture	92
The Lawn, How to Make and Manage—Illustrated	93-97
Flowers, Notes on Their Culture—Illustrated	98-103
Calendar of Garden Operations for the Year	104-106
Conclusion	107

www.ingramcontent.com/pod-product-compliance
Lightning Source LLC
Chambersburg PA
CBHW022147160426
43197CB00009B/1459